פָּרָשַׁת הַשָּׁבוּעַ

Reading Genesis

by Roberta Osser Baum

EDITORIAL COMMITTEE
Rabbi Martin Cohen
Rabbi William Cutter
Rabbi Vicki Lieberman

Behrman House

Project Editors: Gila Gevirtz and Terry Kaye

Book and Cover Design: Dale Moyer

The author and publisher gratefully acknowledge the following sources of photography and art:

Cover: **Creative Image,** foreground; **Richard Lobell,** background

Creative Image, 59, 65, 76; **Jim Cummins/FPG International LLC,** 41; **Francene Keery,** 53; **Larry Nolte,** 56; **Gary Randall/FPG International LLC,** 35; **Gail Shumway/FPG International LLC,** 47; **VCG/FPG International LLC,** 11, 23; **Sunny Yellen,** 29

Copyright © 1999 by Behrman House, Inc.
Springfield, NJ
www.behrmanhouse.com

ISBN 0-87441-680-9

Manufactured in the United States of America

Contents

4	**The Study of Torah**
7	בְּרֵאשִׁית
13	נֹחַ
19	לֶךְ־לְךָ
25	וַיֵּרָא
31	חַיֵּי שָׂרָה
37	תּוֹלְדֹת
43	וַיֵּצֵא
49	וַיִּשְׁלַח
55	וַיֵּשֶׁב
61	מִקֵּץ
67	וַיִּגַּשׁ
73	וַיְחִי

THE STUDY OF TORAH

Turn it again and again, for everything is in it; contemplate it, grow gray and old over it, and swerve not from it, for there is no greater good.
—Ben Bag Bag

The object of the whole Torah is that every person should become a Torah.
—Baal Shem Tov

The Jewish people are dreamers, imaginers of a better, more just, and peaceful world—a world with no war, disease, or hunger; a world filled with love and human kindness. We strive to be faithful to our dream and to its source, God's Torah. We dress the Torah scrolls, respectfully, in plush satins and velvet and adorn them with ornaments made of silver. On the holiday of Shavuot we thank God for giving us the Torah, and on Simḥat Torah we celebrate our yearly reading of the Five Books of Moses by dancing with the Torah. And each week, on Shabbat, we form a great procession proudly carrying the scrolls around the synagogue's sanctuary. But most importantly, we show our love and respect for Torah by studying its ancient stories and laws.

You are an expert at studying. You study subjects as difficult and different as math, history, science, and music. But studying Torah is different. Studying Torah is a mitzvah, a *holy* act. It is how we learn to live as Jews, to live with love, compassion, and respect for God's world. It helps us understand our relationship with God and how we developed as a people. And it guides us as we try to make our dreams for a better world come true.

These are important lessons to learn. That is why we continue to study Torah after we become a bar or bat mitzvah, after we graduate from high school or college, after we marry, have children, find a job, and even after we retire. Our tradition teaches us to study Torah throughout our lives and to study in community so that we can learn from others and share our wisdom.

Each Shabbat we take out a Torah scroll—a *sefer Torah*—from the Holy Ark and read a section of it called the Portion of the Week, or *Parashat Hashavua*. *Parashah* means "portion." Another word for parashah is *sidrah*. The first *parashah* of the yearly cycle begins at the start of Genesis, and the last *parashah* is completed at the end of Deuteronomy. Every year we read all the *parashiyot* (plural of *parashah*) in the same sequence. Beginning with the first *parashah*, we continue, week after week, one *parashah* at a time, until we come to the end of the Five Books of Moses.

Our weekly reading of the Torah is divided into 54 *parashiyot*. Because the number of weeks in the Jewish year varies due to leap years, we combine *parashiyot* as needed. We have a standard way of noting the contents of a *parashah* by listing the book, chapter, and verse (sentence). For example, the first *parashah*, called *Bereishit*, includes Genesis 1:1–6:8. This means it is found in the Book of Genesis, chapter 1, verse 1, through Genesis, chapter 6, verse 8.

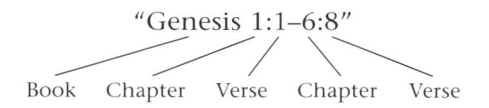

"Genesis 1:1–6:8"
Book   Chapter   Verse   Chapter   Verse

Now you decode where these *parashiyot* are found: *Vayera*, Genesis 18:1–22:24 and *Toldot*, Genesis 25:19–28:9.

During synagogue services, as the person who reads from the Torah scroll chants the *parashah*, the congregants follow along in a *ḥumash*. A Torah scroll is made of parchment, is all in Hebrew, and has no vowels or punctuation—not even periods! In contrast, a *ḥumash* is a book printed on paper with vowels and punctuation. Additionally, a *ḥumash* has the musical notation, or trope, above and below the words to show how to chant the *parashah*, and it usually has an English translation of the Hebrew text. Most *ḥumashim* (plural of *ḥumash*) not only contain the Five Books of Moses, but also include the selections from the Prophets that we read on Shabbat and holidays. Each of these selections is called a *haftarah*.

By reciting the following blessing each time we begin to study Torah, we are reminded that we are about to perform a holy act, an act that should be done with love, respect, and gratitude.

בָּרוּךְ אַתָּה, יְיָ אֱלֹהֵינוּ, מֶלֶךְ הָעוֹלָם,
אֲשֶׁר קִדְּשָׁנוּ בְּמִצְוֹתָיו וְצִוָּנוּ לַעֲסוֹק בְּדִבְרֵי תוֹרָה.

*Praised are You, Adonai our God, Ruler of the universe,
who has made us holy through mitzvot and commands us to engage in the study of Torah.*

בְּרֵאשִׁית נֹחַ לֶךְ־לְךָ וַיֵּרָא חַיֵּי שָׂרָה תּוֹלְדֹת
וַיֵּצֵא וַיִּשְׁלַח וַיֵּשֶׁב מִקֵּץ וַיִּגַּשׁ וַיְחִי

בְּרֵאשִׁית

Genesis 1:1–6:8

בְּרֵאשִׁית בָּרָא אֱלֹהִים אֵת הַשָּׁמַיִם וְאֵת הָאָרֶץ...
וַיֹּאמֶר אֱלֹהִים יְהִי אוֹר וַיְהִי אוֹר:

In the beginning God created the heaven and the earth...and God said, "Let there be light." And there was light. *(Genesis 1:1,3)*

Highlights from Parashat בְּרֵאשִׁית

When God began to create the universe, there was a great darkness. On the first day, God said, "Let there be light," and there was light. God separated the light from the darkness and called the light day, and the darkness night.

On the second day, God created the sky. It separated the waters so that there were waters above and below the sky. On the third day, God created the land, seas, and plants, and on the fourth day, the sun and the moon. On the fifth day, God created birds and fish. And on the sixth day, cattle, reptiles, and wild beasts. On that same day, the sixth day, God created humankind—male and female—in the image of God. And God blessed them. And on the seventh day, God stopped all work and rested. And God declared the seventh day holy.

The man was named Adam, and the woman Eve. They lived in the Garden of Eden, where God said they could eat from every tree except the Tree of Knowledge of Good and Evil. But one day, the serpent tempted Eve to eat fruit from the forbidden tree. After eating from it, she gave some to Adam, who also ate from it.

Having committed a wrong, Adam blamed Eve, and Eve blamed the serpent. But God punished all three. The serpent was made to crawl and eat dust from the earth forever. And Adam and Eve were forced out of Eden. No longer were they given food freely like children; instead, they now had to work each day until their deaths.

Two sons, Cain and Abel, were born to Adam and Eve. Cain killed Abel, and God punished Cain, telling him that he would be an endless wanderer on the earth.

Read the Verse

Read aloud the opening verse of *Parashat* בְּרֵאשִׁית and find the Hebrew word for which the *parashah* is named. Write the name of the *parashah*. _____

Torah Words

אוֹר	הַשָׁמַיִם	בְּרֵאשִׁית
light	the heaven	in the beginning
	הָאָרֶץ	בָּרָא
	the earth	created

In Your Own Words
Read "Highlights from *Parashat* בְּרֵאשִׁית," then retell the story of the first day of Creation using the Torah words above.

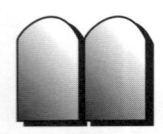

Torah Fact

Each *parashah* is named for the first important word in the first verse of the *parashah*. Similarly, each of the five books of the Torah is named in Hebrew for the first important word in the first verse of that book. For example, the name of the first *parashah* in Genesis is בְּרֵאשִׁית, and the Hebrew name of the Book of Genesis is also בְּרֵאשִׁית.

Parashah People

Read the Hebrew names aloud. Write each one next to its matching English name.

חַוָּה   קַיִן   אָדָם   הֶבֶל

Eve _____   Adam _____

Abel _____   Cain _____

Evening and Morning

The Torah says at the end of each day of Creation, "And there was evening and there was morning," and then names the day. Read the concluding Hebrew phrases.

DAY   DAY

1. וַיְהִי עֶרֶב וַיְהִי בֹקֶר יוֹם אֶחָד   4. וַיְהִי עֶרֶב וַיְהִי בֹקֶר יוֹם רְבִיעִי

2. וַיְהִי עֶרֶב וַיְהִי בֹקֶר יוֹם שֵׁנִי   5. וַיְהִי עֶרֶב וַיְהִי בֹקֶר יוֹם חֲמִישִׁי

3. וַיְהִי עֶרֶב וַיְהִי בֹקֶר יוֹם שְׁלִישִׁי   6. וַיְהִי עֶרֶב וַיְהִי בֹקֶר יוֹם הַשִּׁשִּׁי

Think About It!

Why, according to Jewish tradition, does every day begin in the evening?

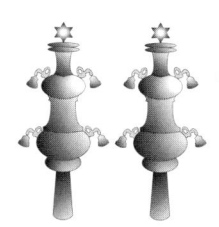

Verses from Parashat בְּרֵאשִׁית

Read these verses from *Parashat* בְּרֵאשִׁית, which describe the seventh day. Then answer the questions.

1. וַיְכֻלּוּ הַשָּׁמַיִם וְהָאָרֶץ...

And the heaven and the earth were finished... (Genesis 2:1)

In what ways is Creation never really completed?

_____

_____

2. ...וַיִּשְׁבֹּת בַּיּוֹם הַשְּׁבִיעִי מִכָּל מְלַאכְתּוֹ אֲשֶׁר עָשָׂה.

...and God rested on the seventh day from all the work that God had done. (Genesis 2:2)

What do you create during the first six days of the week? What can you do to rest and relax on שַׁבָּת?

_____

_____

3. ...וַיְבָרֶךְ אֱלֹהִים אֶת יוֹם הַשְּׁבִיעִי וַיְקַדֵּשׁ אֹתוֹ...

And God blessed the seventh day and made it holy... (Genesis 2:3)

What can you do to help add to the holiness of שַׁבָּת?

_____

A Root: ב ר א

The root ב ר א means "create."

- Write the root. _____ _____ _____   What does it mean? _____

- Read the words built on the root ב ר א. Circle the three root letters in each word.

בָּרָא   וַיִּבְרָא   וּבוֹרֵא

Two of the words appear in the phrases below from *Parashat* בְּרֵאשִׁית.

Find and circle them. Do you recognize the first verse in *Parashat* בְּרֵאשִׁית?

Write the line number. _____

1. בְּרֵאשִׁית בָּרָא אֱלֹהִים אֵת הַשָּׁמַיִם וְאֵת הָאָרֶץ

2. וַיִּבְרָא אֱלֹהִים אֶת הָאָדָם בְּצַלְמוֹ

3. כִּי בוֹ שָׁבַת מִכָּל מְלַאכְתּוֹ אֲשֶׁר בָּרָא אֱלֹהִים לַעֲשׂוֹת

We Praise God

Our tradition teaches us to praise God, the Creator. Read the blessings we recite before eating foods that are not part of a meal, for example, snack foods.

בָּרוּךְ אַתָּה, יְיָ אֱלֹהֵינוּ, מֶלֶךְ הָעוֹלָם...

Praised are You, Adonai our God, Ruler of the universe...

who creates the fruit of the vine	בּוֹרֵא פְּרִי הַגָּפֶן
who creates the fruit of the tree	בּוֹרֵא פְּרִי הָעֵץ
who creates the fruit of the earth	בּוֹרֵא פְּרִי הָאֲדָמָה
who creates many kinds of foods (blessing for grains)	בּוֹרֵא מִינֵי מְזוֹנוֹת

Torah Reading

The following verses are taken from Genesis 2:1–3. They describe how God finished creating the earth, rested on the seventh day, and made the seventh day holy.

וַיְכֻלּוּ הַשָּׁמַיִם וְהָאָרֶץ וְכָל צְבָאָם: וַיְכַל אֱלֹהִים בַּיּוֹם הַשְּׁבִיעִי מְלַאכְתּוֹ אֲשֶׁר עָשָׂה וַיִּשְׁבֹּת בַּיּוֹם הַשְּׁבִיעִי מִכָּל מְלַאכְתּוֹ אֲשֶׁר עָשָׂה: וַיְבָרֶךְ אֱלֹהִים אֶת יוֹם הַשְּׁבִיעִי וַיְקַדֵּשׁ אֹתוֹ כִּי בוֹ שָׁבַת מִכָּל מְלַאכְתּוֹ אֲשֶׁר בָּרָא אֱלֹהִים לַעֲשׂוֹת:

The Mitzvah Connection

In the Image of God בְּצֶלֶם אֱלֹהִים

וַיִּבְרָא אֱלֹהִים אֶת הָאָדָם בְּצַלְמוֹ
בְּצֶלֶם אֱלֹהִים בָּרָא אֹתוֹ
זָכָר וּנְקֵבָה בָּרָא אֹתָם:

And God created humans in God's image, in the image of God, they were created, male and female. (Genesis 1:27)

Sometimes we do not see ourselves as we really are. We may be overly critical and see only our flaws, or we may imagine that we are better and more important than other people. But the truth is, though none of us is perfect, each of us is created in God's image: capable of goodness and worthy of respect.

Read aloud the Hebrew verse and its English translation. Because God has no physical form, to be created in God's image cannot mean that people look like God. It means that we are all born with the ability to follow in God's merciful and loving ways. For example, when we perform the מִצְוָה of giving צְדָקָה by donating money to help feed the hungry, we are following in God's compassionate ways. And when we perform acts of loving-kindness, גְּמִילוּת חֲסָדִים, we reflect God's image. What act of loving-kindness can you perform to show that you are made in God's image, בְּצֶלֶם אֱלֹהִים?

✦ **My Reflections on the Parashah** ✦

בְּרֵאשִׁית נֹחַ לֶךְ־לְךָ וַיֵּרָא חַיֵּי שָׂרָה תּוֹלְדֹת וַיֵּצֵא וַיִּשְׁלַח וַיֵּשֶׁב מִקֵּץ וַיִּגַּשׁ וַיְחִי

נֹחַ

Genesis 6:9-11:32

אֵלֶּה תּוֹלְדֹת נֹחַ נֹחַ אִישׁ צַדִּיק תָּמִים הָיָה בְּדֹרֹתָיו אֶת־הָאֱלֹהִים הִתְהַלֶּךְ־נֹחַ:

These are the generations of Noah. In his generation, Noah was a righteous man and faultless. Noah walked with God. *(Genesis 6:9)*

Highlights from Parashat נֹחַ

Noah was a righteous man who walked with God. But the earth was filled with lawlessness and God therefore decided to destroy the earth and all who lived upon it. God told Noah of the plan and told him to build an ark for himself, his family, and at least two of every animal —one male and one female—and to prepare food for his household and for the animals.

Noah did as God commanded. And the flood came. It rained for forty days and forty nights. The great oceans swelled and increased, until they completely covered the earth. All life that had once existed on dry land was destroyed, except for Noah and those with him, who remained safe in the ark.

The rain stopped and the waters began to recede. Three times Noah sent a dove out from the ark. The first time, the dove could not find a dry resting place. The second time, it brought back an olive leaf in its beak as a sign that dry land had appeared. The third time it did not return at all.

God established a covenant, an agreement, with Noah, his descendants, and all living creatures. Never again would God create a flood to destroy the world. God placed a rainbow in the sky as a sign of the covenant.

Noah, his children, and their descendants inhabited the earth once more. The people grew great in numbers. They decided to build a city with a great tower to reach heaven. Displeased, God decreed that each clan should have its own language and would not understand the other clans. Then God scattered the people over the face of the earth. The tower became known as the Tower of Babel, which means the "Tower of Confusion."

Read the Verse

Read aloud the opening verse of *Parashat* נֹחַ and find the Hebrew word for which the *parashah* is named. Write the name of the *parashah*. _____

Torah Words

קֶשֶׁת
rainbow

יוֹנָה
dove

אִישׁ צַדִּיק
righteous man

בְּרִית
covenant

תֵּבָה
ark

In Your Own Words
Read "Highlights from *Parashat* נֹחַ," then retell the story of the *parashah* using the Torah words above.

Think About It!
What connections do you see between the story of the flood and the story of the Tower of Babel?

A Root: צ ד ק

The root צ ד ק means "justice" and "righteousness."

- Write the root. ___ ___ ___   What does it mean? _____ _____

- Read the words built on the root צ ד ק. Circle the three root letters in each word.

צוֹדֵק   צְדָקָה   צֶדֶק   צַדִּיק   צִדְקַת   צַדִּיקִים

The *parashah* says נֹחַ was a righteous man, that he was אִישׁ צַדִּיק. Find and circle the Hebrew phrase אִישׁ צַדִּיק in the introductory verse of *Parashat* נֹחַ on page 13.

Verses from Parashat נֹחַ

Read these verses from *Parashat* נֹחַ. Then answer the questions.

1. וַיֹּאמֶר אֱלֹהִים לְנֹחַ...כִּי מָלְאָה הָאָרֶץ חָמָס...עֲשֵׂה לְךָ תֵּבַת עֲצֵי גֹפֶר...

   And God said to Noah…"because the earth is filled with lawlessness…make an ark of gopher wood…." (Genesis 6:13–14)

   The Hebrew word תֵּבָה, meaning "ark" or "basket," is used in only one other place in the Torah, in the story of Moses. When he was an infant, Moses' mother placed him in a wicker basket and set it on the Nile River. What do you think the connection is between these two stories?

   _____

   _____

2. ... וַיֵּדַע נֹחַ כִּי קַלּוּ הַמַּיִם מֵעַל הָאָרֶץ.

   …and Noah knew that the waters had receded from the earth. (Genesis 8:11)

   In what ways can the waters of the flood be seen as a symbol of cleansing and new beginnings?

   _____

   _____

3. אֶת קַשְׁתִּי נָתַתִּי בֶּעָנָן וְהָיְתָה לְאוֹת בְּרִית בֵּינִי וּבֵין הָאָרֶץ.

   "I have set my bow (rainbow) in the cloud, and it shall be a sign of a covenant between Me and the earth." (Genesis 9:13)

   What is the covenant this verse refers to? Why do you think God chose the rainbow to be a sign of the covenant?

   _____

   _____

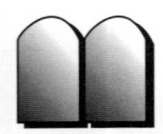

Torah Fact

Below are the names of the five books of the Torah. Can you recite the Hebrew and English names by memory?

Genesis	בְּרֵאשִׁית
Exodus	שְׁמוֹת
Leviticus	וַיִּקְרָא
Numbers	בְּמִדְבַּר
Deuteronomy	דְּבָרִים

Rhythm Reading

When ח comes at the end of a word, the vowel is read *first*. We say "ach."
Write the vowel (ַ) first and then the letter ח to complete each word below.
Read the completed words, and then circle Noah's name.

נֹ___ לוּ___ רוּ___

אוֹר___ שׁוֹל___ מְשַׁמֵּ___

A Covenant, בְּרִית

A covenant–בְּרִית–is an agreement. A rainbow is a sign of the בְּרִית between God and all living creatures. We recite a blessing–בְּרָכָה–when we see a rainbow.

בָּרוּךְ אַתָּה, יְיָ אֱלֹהֵינוּ, מֶלֶךְ הָעוֹלָם,
זוֹכֵר הַבְּרִית וְנֶאֱמָן בִּבְרִיתוֹ וְקַיָּם בְּמַאֲמָרוֹ.

Praised are You, Adonai our God, Ruler of the universe,
who remembers the covenant and is faithful to the covenant and keeps Your promise.

Torah Reading

The following verses are taken from Genesis 8:8–11. They describe how the dove Noah sent from the ark returned with an olive leaf in its beak.

8 וַיְשַׁלַּח אֶת הַיּוֹנָה מֵאִתּוֹ לִרְאוֹת הֲקַלּוּ הַמַּיִם מֵעַל פְּנֵי
9 הָאֲדָמָה: וְלֹא מָצְאָה הַיּוֹנָה מָנוֹחַ לְכַף רַגְלָהּ וַתָּשָׁב אֵלָיו אֶל הַתֵּבָה כִּי מַיִם עַל פְּנֵי כָל הָאָרֶץ וַיִּשְׁלַח יָדוֹ וַיִּקָּחֶהָ וַיָּבֵא
10 אֹתָהּ אֵלָיו אֶל הַתֵּבָה: וַיָּחֶל עוֹד שִׁבְעַת יָמִים אֲחֵרִים וַיֹּסֶף
11 שַׁלַּח אֶת הַיּוֹנָה מִן הַתֵּבָה: וַתָּבֹא אֵלָיו הַיּוֹנָה לְעֵת עֶרֶב וְהִנֵּה עֲלֵה זַיִת טָרָף בְּפִיהָ וַיֵּדַע נֹחַ כִּי קַלּוּ הַמַּיִם מֵעַל הָאָרֶץ:

The Mitzvah Connection

Justice צֶדֶק

צֶדֶק צֶדֶק תִּרְדֹּף...

Justice, justice shall you pursue...
(Deuteronomy 16:20)

These Jews are pursuing justice by protesting acts of racism and anti-Semitism.

Read aloud the Hebrew verse and its English translation. The Torah tells us to be righteous by performing acts of justice–צֶדֶק–acts that make the world just for all God's creations. What can you do to become a more righteous person, אִישׁ צַדִּיק or אִשָּׁה צַדֶּקֶת?

_____

_____

✦ *My Reflections on the Parashah* ✦

אברהם

ישמעאל

הגר

god heard
אלהים שמע

יצחק

Jews

Arabs

בְּרֵאשִׁית   נֹחַ   לֶךְ־לְךָ   וַיֵּרָא   חַיֵּי שָׂרָה   תּוֹלְדֹת
וַיֵּצֵא   וַיִּשְׁלַח   וַיֵּשֶׁב   מִקֵּץ   וַיִּגַּשׁ   וַיְחִי

לֶךְ־לְךָ
Genesis 12:1–17:27

וַיֹּאמֶר יְהוָה אֶל אַבְרָם לֶךְ־לְךָ מֵאַרְצְךָ וּמִמּוֹלַדְתְּךָ וּמִבֵּית אָבִיךָ אֶל הָאָרֶץ אֲשֶׁר אַרְאֶךָּ:

And Adonai said to Abram: "Go forth from your native land and from your father's home to the land that I will show you." *(Genesis 12:1)*

Highlights from Parashat לֶךְ־לְךָ

Almost three hundred years after the flood, a man named Teraḥ had a son called Abram. God told Abram to leave his father's home in Ḥaran and go to a land that God would show him. God said, "I will make of you a great nation, and I will bless you."

Abram and his wife, Sarai, set out on the journey with their nephew, Lot. Lot settled in the plain of the Jordan near the city of Sodom, and Abram settled in Canaan. God promised Abram that all the land that he could see before him God would give to him and to his descendants forever. God also promised Abram, who was childless, that his descendants would be as numerous as the dust of the earth.

Sarai gave her handmaiden, Hagar, to Abram to have a child with him. However, when Hagar became pregnant, Sarai treated her harshly. But God showed mercy to Hagar, and her child was named Ishmael, meaning "God has heard your suffering."

When Abram was ninety-nine years old, God made an everlasting covenant with him and his descendants. God renamed Abram, Abraham, and Sarai, Sarah. God said, "I will make you exceedingly fertile and make nations of you." And God again promised the land of Canaan as an everlasting possession.

God commanded that Abraham and the males of his household be circumcised as a sign of the covenant. God also commanded that all Abraham's male descendants be circumcised on the eighth day following their birth. And God promised to bless Sarah with a son, Isaac, and to keep the covenant with her son.

Abraham did as God commanded. He circumcised himself, Ishmael, and all the men of his household.

Read the Verse

Read aloud the opening verse of *Parashat* לֶךְ־לְךָ and find the Hebrew word for which the *parashah* is named. Write the name of the *parashah*. _____

Torah Words

בְּרִית עוֹלָם	בְּרָכָה	לֶךְ־לְךָ
everlasting covenant	blessing	go
	בָּרוּךְ	הָאָרֶץ
	blessed	the land

In Your Own Words

Read "Highlights from *Parashat* לֶךְ־לְךָ," then, using the Torah words above, retell the story of Abraham's relationship with God.

A Root: ה ל כ

The root ה ל כ means "go" and "walk."

- Write the root. ____ ____ ____ What does it mean? ____ ____

- Sometimes a root letter is missing from a word. Read the following words built on the root ה ל כ. Which root letter is missing?

לֶךְ־לְךָ   וַיֵּלֶךְ   לָלֶכֶת

- Read the verse below from *Parashat* לֶךְ־לְךָ, then circle the words built on the root ה ל כ.

וַיֵּלֶךְ אַבְרָם כַּאֲשֶׁר דִּבֶּר אֵלָיו יְהוָֹה וַיֵּלֶךְ אִתּוֹ לוֹט...

וַיִּקַּח אַבְרָם אֶת שָׂרַי אִשְׁתּוֹ וְאֶת לוֹט בֶּן אָחִיו...

וַיֵּצְאוּ לָלֶכֶת אַרְצָה כְּנָעַן...

And Abram went just as Adonai had told him, and Lot went with him....
And Abram took Sarai, his wife, and Lot, his brother's son...
and they went forth to go to the land of Canaan... (Genesis 12:4–5)

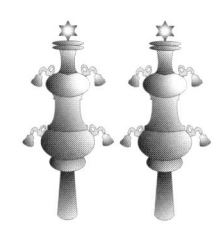

Verses from Parashat לֶךְ־לְךָ

Through a series of promises in *Parashat* לֶךְ־לְךָ God makes an everlasting covenant with Abraham and his descendants. Read each promise below.

1. וְאֶעֶשְׂךָ לְגוֹי גָּדוֹל וַאֲבָרֶכְךָ וַאֲגַדְּלָה שְׁמֶךָ וֶהְיֵה בְּרָכָה.

   "And I will make you a great nation, and I will bless you, and I will make your name great, and you shall be a blessing." (Genesis 12:2)

2. ...שָׂא נָא עֵינֶיךָ וּרְאֵה מִן הַמָּקוֹם אֲשֶׁר אַתָּה שָׁם...כִּי אֶת כָּל הָאָרֶץ אֲשֶׁר אַתָּה רֹאֶה לְךָ אֶתְּנֶנָּה וּלְזַרְעֲךָ עַד עוֹלָם.

   "...Lift your eyes and look from where you are now.... For all the land that you see I will give to you and your descendants forever." (Genesis 13:14–15)

3. ...אַל תִּירָא אַבְרָם אָנֹכִי מָגֵן לָךְ שְׂכָרְךָ הַרְבֵּה מְאֹד.

   "...Fear not, Abram, I am your shield. Your reward shall be very great." (Genesis 15:1)

4. ...כִּי אִם אֲשֶׁר יֵצֵא מִמֵּעֶיךָ הוּא יִירָשֶׁךָ...הַבֶּט נָא הַשָּׁמַיְמָה וּסְפֹר הַכּוֹכָבִים...כֹּה יִהְיֶה זַרְעֶךָ.

   "...none but your very own child shall be your heir.... Look toward the heavens and count the stars...that is how numerous your descendants will be." (Genesis 15:4–5)

How might these promises have helped to strengthen Abraham and Sarah as they made a new life far from their family and friends?

_____

_____

To Be a Blessing

God told Abraham he would be a blessing. What does it mean to *be* a blessing?

_____

Think About It!
To whom would you most like to be a blessing, and why? What can you do to be a blessing?

The Covenant: בְּרִית

Parashat לֶךְ־לְךָ concludes with God establishing an everlasting בְּרִית with Abraham and his descendants. Read the Hebrew selections below from Genesis 17 and read the English translations.

1. אֲנִי אֵל שַׁדַּי הִתְהַלֵּךְ לְפָנַי וֶהְיֵה תָמִים

"I am God Almighty; walk before me and be blameless"

2. וְהָיִיתָ לְאַב הֲמוֹן גּוֹיִם

"and you shall be the father of a multitude of nations"

3. וְהָיָה שִׁמְךָ אַבְרָהָם

"and your name shall be Abraham"

4. שָׂרַי אִשְׁתְּךָ...שָׂרָה שְׁמָהּ

"Sarai your wife...her name shall be Sarah"

What must Abraham do to fulfill the בְּרִית?

_____

_____

Torah Fact

Several people's names are changed in the Torah as a result of their new relationship with God. Describe the new relationship between God and Abraham and Sarah.

_____

_____

Torah Reading

The following verses are taken from Genesis 12:4–7. They describe how Abram and Sarai set out with Lot on their journey to Canaan.

4 וַיֵּלֶךְ אַבְרָם כַּאֲשֶׁר דִּבֶּר אֵלָיו יְהוָֹה וַיֵּלֶךְ אִתּוֹ לוֹט וְאַבְרָם

5 בֶּן חָמֵשׁ שָׁנִים וְשִׁבְעִים שָׁנָה בְּצֵאתוֹ מֵחָרָן: וַיִּקַּח אַבְרָם אֶת שָׂרַי אִשְׁתּוֹ וְאֶת לוֹט בֶּן אָחִיו וְאֶת כָּל רְכוּשָׁם אֲשֶׁר רָכָשׁוּ וְאֶת הַנֶּפֶשׁ אֲשֶׁר עָשׂוּ בְחָרָן וַיֵּצְאוּ לָלֶכֶת אַרְצָה כְּנַעַן

6 וַיָּבֹאוּ אַרְצָה כְּנָעַן: וַיַּעֲבֹר אַבְרָם בָּאָרֶץ עַד מְקוֹם שְׁכֶם עַד אֵלוֹן מוֹרֶה וְהַכְּנַעֲנִי אָז בָּאָרֶץ:

7 וַיֵּרָא יְהוָֹה אֶל אַבְרָם וַיֹּאמֶר לְזַרְעֲךָ אֶתֵּן אֶת הָאָרֶץ הַזֹּאת וַיִּבֶן שָׁם מִזְבֵּחַ לַיהוָֹה הַנִּרְאֶה אֵלָיו:

The Mitzvah Connection

A Good Name שֵׁם טוֹב

שְׁלֹשָׁה כְתָרִים הֵם: כֶּתֶר תּוֹרָה,
וְכֶתֶר כְּהֻנָּה, וְכֶתֶר מַלְכוּת.
וְכֶתֶר שֵׁם טוֹב עוֹלֶה עַל גַּבֵּיהֶן.

There are three crowns: the crown of Torah, the crown of priesthood, and the crown of royalty. But the crown of a good name excels them all. (Pirke Avot 4:17)

A perfect game may be possible when we bowl one strike after another. But living life well is more difficult and complex. That is why our tradition does not require us to be perfect. It simply asks us to aim for our best and to strive for improvement.

Read aloud the Hebrew verse and its English translation. God changed the names of Abram and Sarai by adding the letter *hey* to indicate a new relationship with God. The *hey* symbolizes God's name. Abram and Sarai were entering upon a new relationship with God. Their names and reputations would be passed down throughout the generations as a blessing. Why do you think our tradition teaches us to value the good names and memory of those who came before us?

✦ My Reflections on the Parashah ✦

→ not in Torah

אל
יהי
תהת

בְּרֵאשִׁית נֹחַ לֶךְ־לְךָ וַיֵּרָא חַיֵּי שָׂרָה תּוֹלְדֹת
וַיֵּצֵא וַיִּשְׁלַח וַיֵּשֶׁב מִקֵּץ וַיִּגַּשׁ וַיְחִי

וַיֵּרָא

Genesis 18:1–22:24

וַיֵּרָא אֵלָיו יְהֹוָה בְּאֵלֹנֵי מַמְרֵא וְהוּא יֹשֵׁב פֶּתַח הָאֹהֶל כְּחֹם הַיּוֹם:

And Adonai appeared to him by the oaks of Mamre [an area near Hebron] as he sat in the opening of the tent in the heat of the day. *(Genesis 18:1)*

Highlights from Parashat וַיֵּרָא

God appeared before Abraham in Mamre. Abraham saw three men near his tent. He ran to them and extended hospitality by offering them food, drink, and a place to rest. Sarah helped by making cakes. When she overheard one of the men foretell that she would give birth to a son, Sarah laughed to herself, for she was very old.

Abraham accompanied his guests when they went toward Sodom. The sins of Sodom and Gemorrah were great, and so God threatened to destroy the cities. But Abraham pleaded for God's compassion. He asked if God would spare the city if there were fifty righteous people in it. "Yes!" God answered. Then Abraham asked, what if there were forty-five righteous people; then forty; then thirty; then twenty; and finally ten. Each time God said, "Yes," the city would be saved if these righteous people could be found. And Abraham returned to his home.

Abraham's nephew, Lot, lived in Sodom. When two angels in the form of men arrived there, Lot showed them hospitality. They told him they were about to destroy the city and that Lot must take his family and flee without looking back. They fled, but Lot's wife looked back, and she was turned into a pillar of salt. The next morning, Abraham saw the smoke of destruction rising from Sodom and Gemorrah.

Sarah gave birth to Isaac. When Isaac grew up, God put Abraham to a test. God told Abraham to go and bring Isaac to the land of Moriah and to make a sacrificial offering of him on a mountain there. Abraham obeyed, but as he was about to slay his son on the altar, an angel of God told him not to harm Isaac. In place of Isaac, Abraham sacrificed a ram. The angel declared that Abraham would be blessed and his descendants would be as numerous as the stars of heaven and the sands of the shore.

Read the Verse

Read aloud the opening verse of *Parashat* וַיֵּרָא and find the Hebrew word for which the *parashah* is named. Write the name of the *parashah*. _____

Torah Words

שְׁלֹשָׁה אֲנָשִׁים
three men

סְדֹם
Sodom

חֲמִשִּׁים צַדִּיקִם
fifty righteous people

מַלְאָכִים
angels

In Your Own Words

Read "Highlights from *Parashat* וַיֵּרָא," then, using the Torah words above, describe the bargain Abraham made with God.

A Root: צ ח ק

The root צ ח ק means "laugh."

- Write the root. ____ ____ ____   What does it mean? _____

- Draw a smiling face over the words built on the root צ ח ק in the following selections. Then read each word that has a smile. Read each complete line.

1. וַתִּצְחַק שָׂרָה בְּקִרְבָּהּ...

And Sarah laughed to herself... (Genesis 18:12)

2. וַיֹּאמֶר יְהֹוָה אֶל אַבְרָהָם:
לָמָּה זֶּה צָחֲקָה שָׂרָה...?

And Adonai said to Abraham:
"Why is Sarah laughing...?" (Genesis 18:13)

3. וַתֹּאמֶר שָׂרָה צְחֹק עָשָׂה לִי אֱלֹהִים

And Sarah said, "God made laughter for me..." (Genesis 21:6)

Think About It!

Why do you think Sarah's son was given the name יִצְחָק?

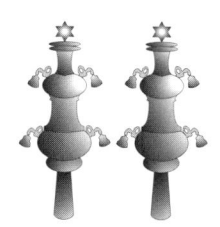

Verses from Parashat וַיֵּרָא

Read these verses from *Parashat* וַיֵּרָא. Then answer the questions.

1. וַיַּשְׁקֵף עַל פְּנֵי סְדֹם וַעֲמֹרָה...עָלָה קִיטֹר הָאָרֶץ כְּקִיטֹר הַכִּבְשָׁן.

   And he (Abraham) looked out toward Sodom and Gemorrah…and behold the smoke of the land went up as the smoke of a furnace. (Genesis 19:28)

   We try to understand events and feelings not described in the Torah. How do you think Abraham felt when he saw Sodom and Gemorrah going up in smoke?

   _____

   _____

2. וַיִּקְרָא אַבְרָהָם אֶת שֶׁם בְּנוֹ...אֲשֶׁר יָלְדָה לוֹ שָׂרָה, יִצְחָק.

   And Abraham called the name of his son…whom Sarah bore to him, Isaac. (Genesis 21:3)

   In Parashat לֶךְ-לְךָ, God told Abraham that the covenant would be continued through the son born to Sarah. What guidance do you think Abraham and Sarah gave to Isaac for the role he was to take on?

   _____

   _____

3. וַיִּקְרָא אֵלָיו מַלְאַךְ יְהוָֹה מִן הַשָּׁמַיִם וַיֹּאמֶר אַבְרָהָם אַבְרָהָם וַיֹּאמֶר הִנֵּנִי...אַל תִּשְׁלַח יָדְךָ אֶל הַנַּעַר...

   And the angel of Adonai called to him from heaven and said: "Abraham, Abraham." And he said, "Here I am." And the angel said, "Do not raise your hand against the boy…." (Genesis 22:11–12)

   Abraham tried to persuade God to act with compassion toward the people of Sodom. Why do you think he was silent when his own son's life was at stake?

   _____

   _____

Rhythm Reading

The י is not sounded when you read יָו (AHV). The ending יָו sounds like the ending וָ in the word יַחְדָו.

The יָו ending means "his" or "him." Read these ending sounds.

תִיו   נִיו   רִיו   לִיו

Read the words below, then circle the word found in the first verse of Parashat וַיֵרָא.

בָּנָיו   עֵינָיו   אֵלָיו   חֲתָנָיו   אַחֲרָיו   לִזְקֵנָיו

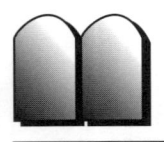

Torah Fact

The word חֻמָשׁ refers to the printed book containing the Five Books of Moses. חֻמָשׁ has the same root ח מ שׁ as the Hebrew word for five: חָמֵשׁ.

Torah Reading

The following verses are taken from Genesis 18:9–13. They describe how Sarah laughed when she overheard one of the messengers tell Abraham that Sarah would give birth to a child in her old age.

9 וַיֹּאמְרוּ אֵלָיו אַיֵּה שָׂרָה אִשְׁתֶּךָ וַיֹּאמֶר הִנֵּה בָאֹהֶל: 10 וַיֹּאמֶר שׁוֹב אָשׁוּב אֵלֶיךָ כָּעֵת חַיָּה וְהִנֵּה בֵן לְשָׂרָה אִשְׁתֶּךָ וְשָׂרָה

11 שֹׁמַעַת פֶּתַח הָאֹהֶל וְהוּא אַחֲרָיו: וְאַבְרָהָם וְשָׂרָה זְקֵנִים

12 בָּאִים בַּיָּמִים חָדַל לִהְיוֹת לְשָׂרָה אֹרַח כַּנָּשִׁים: וַתִּצְחַק שָׂרָה בְּקִרְבָּהּ לֵאמֹר אַחֲרֵי בְלֹתִי הָיְתָה לִּי עֶדְנָה וַאדֹנִי זָקֵן:

13 וַיֹּאמֶר יְהוָה אֶל אַבְרָהָם לָמָּה זֶּה צָחֲקָה שָׂרָה לֵאמֹר הַאַף אֻמְנָם אֵלֵד וַאֲנִי זָקַנְתִּי:

The Mitzvah Connection

Hospitality הַכְנָסַת אוֹרְחִים

וַיִּשָּׂא עֵינָיו וַיַּרְא וְהִנֵּה שְׁלֹשָׁה אֲנָשִׁים נִצָּבִים עָלָיו... וַיָּרָץ לִקְרָאתָם... וַיִּשְׁתַּחוּ אָרְצָה: וַיֹּאמַר... יֻקַּח נָא מְעַט מַיִם וְרַחֲצוּ רַגְלֵיכֶם וְהִשָּׁעֲנוּ תַּחַת הָעֵץ.

And he [Abraham] lifted his eyes and looked, and behold three men stood near him...and he ran to meet them...and he bowed down to the earth. He said "...some water will be brought for you to wash your feet and you may rest under the tree."

(Genesis 18:2–4)

On the holiday of Sukkot we perform the mitzvah of hospitality by inviting family and friends to eat in our sukkah.

Read aloud the Hebrew verses and the English translation above.

Abraham and Sarah were thoughtful and gracious hosts. Read the first paragraph in "Highlights from *Parashat* וַיֵּרָא."

Hospitality is an important Jewish value. In fact, it is a מִצְוָה. In the Passover Haggadah, we read the Aramaic words:

כָּל דִכְפִין יֵיתֵי וְיֵכֹל.

Let all who are hungry come and eat.

How can you observe the מִצְוָה of הַכְנָסַת אוֹרְחִים on שַׁבָּת and holidays?

✦ **My Reflections on the Parashah** ✦

בְּרֵאשִׁית נֹחַ לֶךְ־לְךָ וַיֵּרָא חַיֵּי שָׂרָה תּוֹלְדֹת וַיֵּצֵא וַיִּשְׁלַח וַיֵּשֶׁב מִקֵּץ וַיִּגַּשׁ וַיְחִי

חַיֵּי שָׂרָה

Genesis 23:1–25:18

> וַיִּהְיוּ חַיֵּי שָׂרָה מֵאָה שָׁנָה וְעֶשְׂרִים שָׁנָה וְשֶׁבַע שָׁנִים שְׁנֵי חַיֵּי שָׂרָה: וַתָּמָת שָׂרָה בְּקִרְיַת אַרְבַּע הִוא חֶבְרוֹן בְּאֶרֶץ כְּנָעַן וַיָּבֹא אַבְרָהָם לִסְפֹּד לְשָׂרָה וְלִבְכֹּתָהּ:
>
> And Sarah lived one hundred and seven and twenty years. These were the years of Sarah's life. And Sarah died in Kiryat Arba, which is Hebron, in the land of Canaan, and Abraham came to mourn for Sarah and to weep for her. *(Genesis 23:1–2)*

Highlights from Parashat חַיֵּי שָׂרָה

Sarah died when she was 127 years old. Abraham mourned and cried for her. He went to Ephron, a Hittite, to buy the cave of Machpelah as a burial place. Ephron said he would give Abraham the field and cave of Machpelah but Abraham insisted on paying its full value. He bought the land for 400 shekels of silver and buried Sarah there.

Abraham ordered his senior servant to return to his native land to find a wife for Isaac and bring her back to Canaan. The servant took ten of his master's camels and set out on his mission. When he arrived in the city of Abraham's brother Naḥor, he spoke to God, asking for a sign that would let him know who Isaac's intended wife was. He said, "Let the maiden to whom I say, 'Please, lower your jar that I may drink,' and who answers, 'Drink and I will also give water to your camels,' let her be the one."

Before the servant finished speaking, he saw a beautiful young woman near the well with a water jar on her shoulder. She was Rebecca, granddaughter of Naḥor. "Please let me sip a bit of water from your jar," the servant requested. Rebecca quickly gave him water and let him drink his fill. Then she continued to draw water so that his camels would also have enough to drink.

Rebecca brought Abraham's servant to her family, where he was warmly welcomed into the household of her brother Laban. The servant told the family of his mission, and they asked Rebecca if she wanted to return with him to become Isaac's wife. Rebecca said, "Yes." Her family blessed her, and then she and her maids returned with the servant to Canaan. And Rebecca became Isaac's wife.

Abraham took another wife and he had children with her. But he willed all he owned to Isaac. Abraham lived 175 years. His sons Isaac and Ishmael buried him with Sarah at Machpelah.

Read the Verse

Read aloud the opening verse of *Parashat* חַיֵּי שָׂרָה and find the Hebrew word for which the *parashah* is named. Write the name of the *parashah*. _____

Torah Words

אַרְבַּע מֵאוֹת שֶׁקֶל כֶּסֶף	מְעָרַת הַמַּכְפֵּלָה	חַיֵּי שָׂרָה
400 shekels of silver	cave of Machpelah	the life of Sarah

In Your Own Words
Read "Highlights from *Parashat* חַיֵּי שָׂרָה," then, using the Torah words above, create a dialogue in which Abraham and Ephron discuss the land for Sarah's burial site.

Think About It!
Why do you think Abraham insisted on buying the land and the cave rather than accepting them as gifts?

A Root: ח י ה

The root ח י ה means "life."

- Write the root. ____ ____ ____   What does it mean? _____

- Read the words built on the root ח י ה.

שֶׁהֶחֱיָנוּ   חָיָה   חַיִּים   חַי

- Read the phrases that follow, then circle the name of the *parashah*.

נֶפֶשׁ חַיָּה   חַיֵּי שָׂרָה   אָדָם אֲשֶׁר חַי

Read the following verse from *Parashat* בְּרֵאשִׁית, then circle the words built on the root ח י ה.

וַיִּיצֶר יְהוָה אֱלֹהִים אֶת הָאָדָם עָפָר מִן הָאֲדָמָה
וַיִּפַּח בְּאַפָּיו נִשְׁמַת חַיִּים וַיְהִי הָאָדָם לְנֶפֶשׁ חַיָּה.

*And God formed humans out of the dust of the earth
and breathed into their nostrils the breath of life, and they became living beings.* (Genesis 2:7)

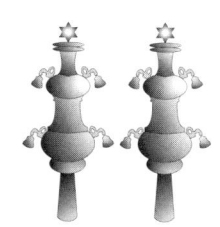

Verses from Parashat חַיֵּי שָׂרָה

Read these verses from Parashat חַיֵּי שָׂרָה, then answer the questions.

1. וְאַבְרָהָם זָקֵן בָּא בַּיָּמִים וַיהֹוָה בֵּרַךְ אֶת אַבְרָהָם בַּכֹּל.

   And Abraham was old, advanced in years, and Adonai had blessed Abraham in everything. (Genesis 24:1)

   In what ways had God blessed Abraham?

   _____
   _____

2. וַיְבָרְכוּ אֶת רִבְקָה וַיֹּאמְרוּ לָהּ אֲחֹתֵנוּ אַתְּ הֲיִי לְאַלְפֵי רְבָבָה...

   And they blessed Rebecca and said to her: "Our sister, may you be the mother of tens of thousands…" (Genesis 24:60)

   Do you think that Rebecca believed her family's blessing would come true? Why or why not?

   _____
   _____

3. וַיִּקְבְּרוּ אֹתוֹ יִצְחָק וְיִשְׁמָעֵאל בָּנָיו אֶל מְעָרַת הַמַּכְפֵּלָה...
   שָׁמָּה קֻבַּר אַבְרָהָם וְשָׂרָה אִשְׁתּוֹ.

   And Isaac and Ishmael, Abraham's sons, buried him in the cave of Machpelah…. There Abraham was buried along with Sarah his wife. (Genesis 25:9–10)

   Why do you think the Torah tells us that Abraham buried Sarah, that Isaac and Ishmael buried Abraham, and that Abraham and Sarah were buried in the same place?

   _____
   _____

A Blessing

The following blessing is recited on the first day of a holiday or on a special occasion or a first-time event, such as a birthday, a graduation, or the first time you ride a new bike. Read the blessing and circle the word built on the root ח י ה.

בָּרוּךְ אַתָּה, יְיָ אֱלֹהֵינוּ, מֶלֶךְ הָעוֹלָם,

שֶׁהֶחֱיָנוּ וְקִיְּמָנוּ וְהִגִּיעָנוּ לַזְּמַן הַזֶּה.

Praised are You, Adonai our God, Ruler of the universe,
who has given us life and sustained us and permitted us to reach this season.

Why do you think we recite this blessing on holidays?

_____

_____

How can reciting a blessing help make a special event more important?

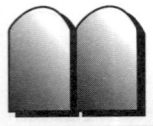

_____

_____

Torah Fact

The term סֵפֶר תּוֹרָה refers to the Torah scroll. A סֵפֶר תּוֹרָה is made of parchment known as קְלָף. The parchment is made of sheepskin or goatskin. The sheets of parchment are sewn together and then attached to wooden rollers called עֲצֵי חַיִּים, "Trees of Life." The Torah, God's Teaching, is known as a Tree of Life, עֵץ חַיִּים.

Think About It!
Why do you think the Torah is called עֵץ חַיִּים? Why do you think the rollers that support the Torah are called עֲצֵי חַיִּים?

Torah Reading

The following verses are taken from Genesis 23:8–11. They describe how Abraham asked to buy the cave of Machpelah from Ephron the Hittite, so that he could bury Sarah.

8 וַיְדַבֵּר אִתָּם לֵאמֹר אִם יֵשׁ אֶת נַפְשְׁכֶם לִקְבֹּר אֶת מֵתִי

9 מִלְּפָנַי שְׁמָעוּנִי וּפִגְעוּ לִי בְּעֶפְרוֹן בֶּן צֹחַר: וְיִתֶּן לִי אֶת מְעָרַת הַמַּכְפֵּלָה אֲשֶׁר לוֹ אֲשֶׁר בִּקְצֵה שָׂדֵהוּ בְּכֶסֶף מָלֵא

10 יִתְּנֶנָּה לִי בְּתוֹכְכֶם לַאֲחֻזַּת קָבֶר: וְעֶפְרוֹן יֹשֵׁב בְּתוֹךְ בְּנֵי חֵת וַיַּעַן עֶפְרוֹן הַחִתִּי אֶת אַבְרָהָם בְּאָזְנֵי בְנֵי חֵת

11 לְכֹל בָּאֵי שַׁעַר עִירוֹ לֵאמֹר: לֹא אֲדֹנִי שְׁמָעֵנִי הַשָּׂדֶה נָתַתִּי לָךְ וְהַמְּעָרָה אֲשֶׁר בּוֹ לְךָ נְתַתִּיהָ...

The Mitzvah Connection

Kindness to Animals צַעַר בַּעֲלֵי חַיִּים

וַתְּכַל לְהַשְׁקֹתוֹ וַתֹּאמֶר
גַּם לִגְמַלֶּיךָ אֶשְׁאָב
עַד אִם כִּלּוּ לִשְׁתֹּת.

And when she [Rebecca] let him [the servant] drink his fill, she said: "I will also draw water for your camels until they have had enough to drink." (Genesis 24:19)

Our tradition teaches us to study the Torah all the days of our lives. One reason is to remind us to not only enjoy the goodness and beauty of Creation, but also to care for God's other creatures.

Read aloud the Hebrew verse and its English translation. Throughout the Torah there are teachings about kindness to animals. For example, Exodus and Deuteronomy teach that on Shabbat not only people, but their animals as well, are to rest. Deuteronomy also teaches that it is forbidden to plow with an ox and a donkey harnessed together. Because oxen are larger and more powerful than donkeys, it would be cruel to force a donkey to work as hard as an ox. In what ways can people care for their pets and for other animals, such as those living in zoos or forests?

✦ My Reflections on the Parashah ✦

- Abraham --- אברהם
- Isaac --- יצחק
- Rebecca --- רבקה
- Betuel (M) --- בתואל
- Laban (M) --- לבן

בְּרֵאשִׁית נֹחַ לֶךְ־לְךָ וַיֵּרָא חַיֵּי שָׂרָה **תּוֹלְדֹת**
וַיֵּצֵא וַיִּשְׁלַח וַיֵּשֶׁב מִקֵּץ וַיִּגַּשׁ וַיְחִי

תּוֹלְדֹת

Genesis 25:19–28:9

וְאֵלֶּה תּוֹלְדֹת יִצְחָק בֶּן־אַבְרָהָם אַבְרָהָם הוֹלִיד אֶת־יִצְחָק:
וַיְהִי יִצְחָק בֶּן־אַרְבָּעִים שָׁנָה בְּקַחְתּוֹ אֶת־רִבְקָה בַּת־בְּתוּאֵל
הָאֲרַמִּי מִפַּדַּן אֲרָם אֲחוֹת לָבָן הָאֲרַמִּי לוֹ לְאִשָּׁה:

And these are the generations of Isaac, Abraham's son: Abraham fathered Isaac. And Isaac was forty years old when he married Rebecca, the daughter of Bethuel the Aramean of Paddan-aram, the sister of Laban the Aramean. *(Genesis 25:19–20)*

Highlights from Parashat תּוֹלְדֹת

This is the story of the descendants of Isaac, son of Abraham and Sarah. God told Rebecca, Isaac's wife, that she would have twin sons, who would become two separate nations, the older one serving the younger. As the firstborn—Esau—came out of Rebecca's womb, the second born—Jacob—grasped the heel of his brother's foot.

When the twins grew up, Esau became a skillful hunter and Jacob became a mild man who preferred the indoors. One day, Esau came home from the fields and asked his brother for some of the lentil stew he was cooking. Jacob said he would sell him the stew in exchange for his birthright as the firstborn son. Esau was very hungry, so he agreed, and Jacob gave Esau bread and stew in return for his birthright.

Esau was Isaac's favorite son, but Rebecca favored Jacob. One day, when Isaac was old, Isaac thought he was dying and wanted to bless Esau with the special blessing due the firstborn. While Esau was out hunting for food for Isaac, Rebecca dressed Jacob as Esau. Because Isaac's eyes were too dim to see, Rebecca and Jacob were able to trick him into giving Esau's blessing to Jacob.

Esau threatened to kill Jacob for his trickery. To protect him, Rebecca urged Jacob to go to her brother Laban in Ḥaran and stay there until Esau's anger faded. Isaac instructed Jacob to marry one of Laban's daughters. Isaac blessed Jacob again, saying, "May God grant the blessing of Abraham to you and to your descendants that you may own the land…that God gave to Abraham."

Read the Verse

Read aloud the opening verse of *Parashat* תּוֹלְדֹת and find the Hebrew word for which the *parashah* is named. Write the name of the *parashah*. _____

Torah Words

בְּרָכָה	בְּכֹרָה	תּוֹלְדֹת
blessing	birthright	generations (of)

In Your Own Words
Read "Highlights from *Parashat* תּוֹלְדֹת," then retell the story of the *parashah* using the Torah words above.

Generations

Fill in the blanks with the correct names in English and Hebrew.

Jacob	*Abraham*	*Esau*	*Sarah*	*Isaac*
יַעֲקֹב	אַבְרָהָם	עֵשָׂו	שָׂרָה	יִצְחָק

	ENGLISH	HEBREW
Father	_____	_____
Mother	_____	_____
Son	_____	_____
Grandsons	_____	_____
	_____	_____

Related Words

The Book of Genesis is concerned with continuity through the stories of each generation. It records whom each person marries, who their children are, and the names of those in the generations that follow. Each selection below comes from a verse in Genesis. Read the selections and circle the word in each verse meaning "generations of."

1. זֶה סֵפֶר תּוֹלְדֹת אָדָם
2. אֵלֶּה תּוֹלְדֹת נֹחַ
3. וְאֵלֶּה תּוֹלְדֹת בְּנֵי נֹחַ
4. וְאֵלֶּה תּוֹלְדֹת תֶּרַח
5. וְאֵלֶּה תֹלְדֹת יִשְׁמָעֵאל
6. וְאֵלֶּה תּוֹלְדֹת יִצְחָק
7. אֵלֶּה תֹלְדוֹת יַעֲקֹב

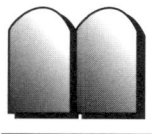

Torah Fact

A סֵפֶר תּוֹרָה is written by a scribe, a סוֹפֵר. The סוֹפֵר copies the Torah text with a feather pen dipped in special black ink. The סוֹפֵר must follow a strict set of rules. For example, the סוֹפֵר may not write from memory and must pronounce each word before writing it. For thousands of years, Torah scrolls have been written in this way.

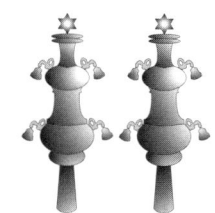

Verses from Parashat תּוֹלְדֹת

Read these verses from *Parashat* תּוֹלְדֹת. Draw a triangle next to the verse that shows that Jacob succeeded in tricking his father. Draw a circle next to the verse that shows God declared which twin would become the leader. Place a box next to the verse that shows that Esau did not value being the leader.

1. שְׁנֵי גוֹיִם בְּבִטְנֵךְ... וְרַב יַעֲבֹד צָעִיר.

"Two nations are in your womb...and the older shall serve the younger." (Genesis 25:23)

2. וַיֹּאמֶר יַעֲקֹב מִכְרָה כַיּוֹם אֶת בְּכֹרָתְךָ לִי... וַיִּמְכֹּר אֶת בְּכֹרָתוֹ לְיַעֲקֹב.

And Jacob said: "Now sell me your birthright"...and he sold his birthright to Jacob. (Genesis 25:31,33)

3. וַיְבָרְכֵהוּ וַיֹּאמֶר...יַעַבְדוּךָ עַמִּים וְיִשְׁתַּחֲווּ לְךָ...וּמְבָרְכֶיךָ בָּרוּךְ.

...and he [Isaac] blessed him [Jacob dressed as Esau] and said: "...Let peoples serve you and nations bow to you...and blessed be those who bless you." (Genesis 27:27,29)

A Root: ב ר כ

The root ב ר כ means "bless" and "praise."

- Write the root. ____ ____ ____   What does it mean? _____ _____

- Read the following words that are built on the root ב ר כ.

בִּרְכַּת יִתְבָּרַךְ בְּרָכָה יְבָרֶכְךָ בְּרָכוֹת

- Read the third selection in "Verses from *Parashat* תּוֹלְדֹת." Circle the three words that are built on the root ב ר כ.

A Prefix: וְ וַ וּ

The prefixes וְ וַ וּ mean "and." Look once again at "Verses from *Parashat* תּוֹלְדֹת." Underline, then read each Hebrew word with a prefix meaning "and."

Root Review

Connect each root to its matching Hebrew word. Then write the English meaning next to each root.

_____	ברכ	בּוֹרֵא
_____	צדק	צְדָקָה
_____	חיה	בָּרוּךְ
_____	צחק	חַיִּים
_____	ברא	יִצְחָק
_____	הלכ	לֵךְ

Torah Reading

The following verses are taken from Genesis 27: 21–24. They describe how Jacob tricked Isaac into giving him Esau's blessing.

21 וַיֹּאמֶר יִצְחָק אֶל יַעֲקֹב גְּשָׁה נָּא וַאֲמֻשְׁךָ בְּנִי הַאַתָּה זֶה
22 בְּנִי עֵשָׂו אִם לֹא: וַיִּגַּשׁ יַעֲקֹב אֶל יִצְחָק אָבִיו וַיְמֻשֵּׁהוּ
23 וַיֹּאמֶר הַקֹּל קוֹל יַעֲקֹב וְהַיָּדַיִם יְדֵי עֵשָׂו: וְלֹא הִכִּירוֹ כִּי הָיוּ
24 יָדָיו כִּידֵי עֵשָׂו אָחִיו שְׂעִרֹת וַיְבָרְכֵהוּ: וַיֹּאמֶר אַתָּה זֶה בְּנִי עֵשָׂו וַיֹּאמֶר אָנִי:

The Mitzvah Connection

Do Not Place a Stumbling Block   לֹא תִתֵּן מִכְשֹׁל

...וְלִפְנֵי עִוֵּר לֹא תִתֵּן מִכְשֹׁל...

...And do not place a stumbling block before the blind.... (Leviticus 19:14)

In basketball it is fair to block our competitors so that they don't succeed. But what if we trick a classmate who is running against us in a school election. Would that be fair? Why or why not?

Read aloud the Hebrew verse and its English translation. The ancient rabbis interpreted this verse to mean that we should not purposefully trick a vulnerable or weak person. Do you think that Rebecca and Jacob placed a stumbling block before Isaac? Explain your answer.

_____

_____

_____

Think About It!
Why do you think the Torah teaches us about the shortcomings as well as the strengths of our patriarchs and matriarchs?

✦ **My Reflections on the Parashah** ✦

בְּרֵאשִׁית נֹחַ לֶךְ-לְךָ וַיֵּרָא חַיֵּי שָׂרָה תּוֹלְדֹת
וַיֵּצֵא וַיִּשְׁלַח וַיֵּשֶׁב מִקֵּץ וַיִּגַּשׁ וַיְחִי

וַיֵּצֵא

Genesis 28:10–32:3

וַיֵּצֵא יַעֲקֹב מִבְּאֵר שָׁבַע וַיֵּלֶךְ חָרָנָה: וַיִּפְגַּע בַּמָּקוֹם וַיָּלֶן שָׁם כִּי בָא הַשֶּׁמֶשׁ וַיִּקַּח מֵאַבְנֵי הַמָּקוֹם וַיָּשֶׂם מְרַאֲשֹׁתָיו וַיִּשְׁכַּב בַּמָּקוֹם הַהוּא: וַיַּחֲלֹם...

Jacob went out from Beer Sheba and went toward Ḥaran. And he came upon the place and stopped there for the night, for the sun had set. And he took one of the stones of the place and put it under his head and slept there. And he had a dream...

(Genesis 28:10–12)

Highlights from Parashat וַיֵּצֵא

Jacob left Beer Sheba and went toward Ḥaran. Stopping to rest for the night, he placed a stone under his head as he lay down. He dreamed that a ladder was set upon the ground, its top reaching the sky. Angels of God were ascending and descending the ladder. And God stood before Jacob saying, "I am Adonai, the God of Abraham and the God of Isaac. I will give the ground you are lying on to you and to your descendants, who will be as numerous as the dust of the earth." God also promised to protect Jacob wherever he would go and to bring him back to this land.

When Jacob awoke, he knew that God had been in that place. He took the stone he had placed under his head and set it up as a marker. He anointed it with oil and named the place Bethel, House of God.

Approaching Ḥaran, Jacob stopped by a well. Laban's daughter, Rachel, came to the well. Jacob helped water her sheep and introduced himself as the son of Rebecca, her father's sister.

Jacob was embraced by Rachel's family. Jacob loved Rachel and worked seven years for Laban so that she would become his wife. But, instead of Rachel, Laban gave Jacob Leah, Rachel's older sister. Jacob was angry at being tricked, but he took Leah as a wife and then Rachel. Therefore, Jacob had to work another seven years for Laban.

In time, Leah and Jacob had six sons and one daughter. Jacob also had four sons with Bilhah and Zilpah, Leah and Rachel's handmaidens. Then, Rachel bore a son, Joseph. [In the next *parashah*, we learn that Rachel had a second son, Benjamin.] Jacob's wealth grew, and he wanted to return to Canaan. So, Jacob, his wives, his children, and all their household left Ḥaran.

Read the Verse

Read aloud the opening verse of *Parashat* וַיֵּצֵא and find the Hebrew word for which the *parashah* is named. Write the name of the *parashah*. _____

Torah Words

בְּאֵר
a well

סֻלָּם
ladder

שֶׁבַע שָׁנִים
seven years

מַלְאֲכֵי אֱלֹהִים
angels of God

In Your Own Words

Read "Highlights from *Parashat* וַיֵּצֵא," then, using the Torah words above, retell the story of Jacob's journey and his life in Ḥaran.

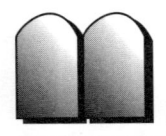

Torah Fact

This is how Hebrew letters are written in a סֵפֶר תּוֹרָה.

אבגדהוזחטיכךלמםנןסעפףצץקרשת

Nine letters of the *alef bet* are decorated with crowns when they are written in a סֵפֶר תּוֹרָה. The crowns are drawn as three vertical lines on the top of the letter. Try to write the letters that have crowns in a סֵפֶר תּוֹרָה.

Become a Torah Reader

וַיֵּצֵא יַעֲקֹב מִבְּאֵר שָׁבַע וַיֵּלֶךְ חָרָנָה.

Jacob went out from Beer Sheba and went toward Ḥaran. (Genesis 28:10)

Read the verse above in Hebrew. This is how it looks in the סֵפֶר תּוֹרָה. Try to read it.

ויצא יעקב מבאר שבע וילך חרנה

Jacob's Ladder

The angels of God, מַלְאֲכֵי אֱלֹהִים, ascended and descended Jacob's ladder. Read these words from Jacob's dream, first in ascending and then in descending order.

6. בַּמָּקוֹם הַזֶּה — in this place
5. יֹרְדִים — descending
4. עֹלִים — ascending
3. הַשָּׁמַיְמָה — to heaven
2. אַרְצָה — on the earth
1. סֻלָּם — ladder

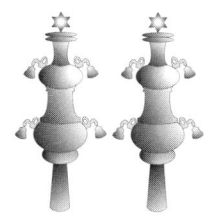

Verses from Parashat וַיֵּצֵא

The verses below describe Jacob's dream. The missing Hebrew words can be found in Jacob's Ladder above. Write them on the appropriate lines, then read each completed Hebrew verse.

1. וַיַּחֲלֹם וְהִנֵּה _____ מֻצָּב _____ וְרֹאשׁוֹ מַגִּיעַ _____...

And he [Jacob] dreamed that a <u>ladder</u> was set up <u>on the earth</u> with its top reaching all the way <u>to heaven</u>... (Genesis 28:12)

2. ...וְהִנֵּה מַלְאֲכֵי אֱלֹהִים _____ וְ_____ בּוֹ.

...and behold the angels of God <u>ascending</u> and <u>descending</u> on it. (Genesis 28:12)

3. וַיִּיקַץ יַעֲקֹב מִשְּׁנָתוֹ וַיֹּאמֶר אָכֵן יֵשׁ יְהוָה _____ _____ וְאָנֹכִי לֹא יָדָעְתִּי.

And Jacob awoke and said: "Surely Adonai is <u>in this place</u>, and I did not know it."

(Genesis 28:16)

Think About It!
Why do you think Jacob said, "Surely Adonai is in this place"?

A Root: ע ב ד

The root ע ב ד means "service." *Service* refers to "work" and "service to God," or "worship."

- Write the root. ____ ____ ____

  What does it mean? _____

- Read the words built on the root ע ב ד.

עֲבוֹדָה   עֲבָדִים   וַיַּעֲבֹד

45

Seven & Seven

Jacob worked seven years and then he worked another seven years. Read the selections from the *parashah*. Circle words built on the root ע ב ד.

"I will serve you seven years for Rachel" 1. אֶעֱבָדְךָ שֶׁבַע שָׁנִים בְּרָחֵל

And Jacob served seven years for Rachel 2. וַיַּעֲבֹד יַעֲקֹב בְּרָחֵל שֶׁבַע שָׁנִים

"For the service that you shall do" 3. בַּעֲבֹדָה אֲשֶׁר תַּעֲבֹד

Which phrase in the above selections means "seven years"? _____

Relationships

God had a personal relationship with each of our patriarchs and matriarchs. Read the Hebrew phrases and write the missing English names on the lines.

אֱלֹהֵי אַבְרָהָם, אֱלֹהֵי יִצְחָק, וֵאלֹהֵי יַעֲקֹב

God of _____, God of _____, and God of _____

אֱלֹהֵי שָׂרָה, אֱלֹהֵי רִבְקָה, אֱלֹהֵי לֵאָה, וֵאלֹהֵי רָחֵל

God of _____, God of _____, God of _____, and God of _____

Think About It!
In prayer, why do you think we say אֱלֹהֵי—God of—before each name, not just at the beginning of the phrase?

Countdown

Learn to count in Hebrew from one to ten.

שֵׁשׁ	6	אַחַת	1
שֶׁבַע	7	שְׁתַּיִם	2
שְׁמוֹנֶה	8	שָׁלֹשׁ	3
תֵּשַׁע	9	אַרְבַּע	4
עֶשֶׂר	10	חָמֵשׁ	5

Try to count from one to ten in Hebrew from memory.

Torah Reading

The following verses are taken from Genesis 28:10–14. They describe how Jacob dreamed that the angels of God were ascending and descending a ladder set upon the ground, its top reaching the sky.

10
11 וַיֵּצֵא יַעֲקֹב מִבְּאֵר שָׁבַע וַיֵּלֶךְ חָרָנָה: וַיִּפְגַּע בַּמָּקוֹם וַיָּלֶן שָׁם כִּי בָא הַשֶּׁמֶשׁ וַיִּקַּח מֵאַבְנֵי הַמָּקוֹם וַיָּשֶׂם מְרַאֲשֹׁתָיו

12 וַיִּשְׁכַּב בַּמָּקוֹם הַהוּא: וַיַּחֲלֹם וְהִנֵּה סֻלָּם מֻצָּב אַרְצָה וְרֹאשׁוֹ מַגִּיעַ הַשָּׁמָיְמָה וְהִנֵּה מַלְאֲכֵי אֱלֹהִים עֹלִים וְיֹרְדִים בּוֹ:

13 וְהִנֵּה יְהוָה נִצָּב עָלָיו וַיֹּאמַר אֲנִי יְהוָה אֱלֹהֵי אַבְרָהָם אָבִיךָ וֵאלֹהֵי יִצְחָק הָאָרֶץ אֲשֶׁר אַתָּה שֹׁכֵב עָלֶיהָ לְךָ

14 אֶתְּנֶנָּה וּלְזַרְעֶךָ: וְהָיָה זַרְעֲךָ כַּעֲפַר הָאָרֶץ וּפָרַצְתָּ יָמָּה וָקֵדְמָה וְצָפֹנָה וָנֶגְבָּה...

The Mitzvah Connection

Tithing מַעֲשֵׂר

...וְכֹל אֲשֶׁר תִּתֶּן לִי עַשֵּׂר אֲעַשְּׂרֶנּוּ לָךְ.

"...and from all that You shall give me I will give a tenth [back] to You." (Genesis 28:22)

Read aloud the Hebrew verse and its translation. Upon awakening from his dream, Jacob made a vow. If God remained with him on his journey and he arrived safely at his father's house, Jacob would give one-tenth of his wealth to God. This promise led to the mitzvah of Jews giving one-tenth of their income to the Temple and to the needy. Do you think it is fair to expect all Jews—both rich and poor—to give one-tenth of their income to support the Jewish community and to help those who are needier than themselves? Why or why not?

Money does not grow on trees. It is a precious resource we must use wisely—not only to meet our own needs and desires, but also to help those who are less fortunate. How can you be sure to set aside money for those in need?

✦ My Reflections on the Parashah ✦

בְּרֵאשִׁית נֹחַ לֶךְ־לְךָ וַיֵּרָא חַיֵּי שָׂרָה תּוֹלְדֹת
וַיֵּצֵא וַיִּשְׁלַח וַיֵּשֶׁב מִקֵּץ וַיִּגַּשׁ וַיְחִי

וַיִּשְׁלַח

Genesis 32:4–36:43

> וַיִּשְׁלַח יַעֲקֹב מַלְאָכִים לְפָנָיו אֶל עֵשָׂו אָחִיו אַרְצָה שֵׂעִיר שְׂדֵה אֱדוֹם: וַיְצַו אֹתָם לֵאמֹר כֹּה תֹאמְרוּן... וָאֶשְׁלְחָה לְהַגִּיד לַאדֹנִי לִמְצֹא חֵן בְּעֵינֶיךָ:
>
> Jacob sent messengers ahead of him to his brother Esau in the land of Seir, in Edom, and he commanded them saying, "Thus shall you say: … 'I [have returned with riches and now] send [this message] to tell my lord [Esau], so that I may earn your favor.'"
>
> *(Genesis 32:4–6)*

Highlights from Parashat וַיִּשְׁלַח

As Jacob neared Canaan, he sent messengers to Seir to tell his brother, Esau, that he was returning with riches. The messengers returned saying that Esau was coming to meet Jacob with 400 men. Fearful, Jacob prayed to God and sent gifts ahead for Esau.

The night before the meeting with Esau was to take place, Jacob sent his family and possessions to the other side of the river Jabbok. He was left by himself. A "man" wrestled with him that night. Jacob overcame the man and refused to let him go unless the man blessed him, which he did by renaming Jacob, Israel. Jacob then named the place Peniel, meaning, "I have seen God face to face, yet my life has been spared."

Jacob continued on his way until he saw his brother, Esau, coming. Jacob approached him, bowing seven times. Esau embraced and kissed his brother, and they both wept. Esau told Jacob there was no need to give him gifts, but Jacob insisted. Finally, Esau returned to Seir, and Jacob continued on his way.

One day, God spoke to Jacob, telling him to return to live in Bethel. There, God renewed the covenant, telling Jacob that a nation would descend from him and that the land God had given to Abraham and Isaac now belonged to him and his offspring. On their way back from Bethel, Rachel gave birth to Benjamin, and then she died. Jacob buried her and set up a pillar to mark the site. Jacob then returned to his father, Isaac, who died at 180 years of age. Isaac's sons, Jacob and Esau, buried Isaac just as Isaac and Ishmael had buried their father, Abraham.

Read the Verse

Read aloud the opening verse of *Parashat* וַיִּשְׁלַח and find the Hebrew word for which the *parashah* is named. Write the name of the *parashah*. _____

Torah Words

בֵּית-אֵל
Bethel

עֵשָׂו וְיַעֲקֹב
Esau and Jacob

וַיֵּאָבֵק אִישׁ עִמּוֹ
and a man wrestled with him

In Your Own Words

Read "Highlights from *Parashat* וַיִּשְׁלַח," then describe these events: Jacob wrestling with "a man" during the night, his encounter with his brother, and his revisiting Bethel. In your descriptions, use the Torah words above.

History Repeats Itself

Jacob had an experience with angels during the night when he left his home twenty years before to go to Ḥaran. Now, upon his return home, Jacob had a nighttime experience in which he wrestled with "a man."

Answer each question twice—first in regard to Jacob's journey to Ḥaran, and then in regard to his journey to Canaan.

1. Whom was Jacob on his way to meet?
2. How do you think Jacob felt when he began his journey? Why?
3. What happened on the journey?
4. How do you think Jacob felt when he arrived at his destination? Why?
5. What promise did God make to Jacob at Bethel on each journey?

GOING TO HARAN *(The Journey Away from Home)*	GOING TO CANAAN *(The Journey Returning Home)*
1.	
2.	
3.	
4.	
5.	

A Root: א מ ר

The root א מ ר means "say" and "speak."

- Write the root. ____ ____ ____   What does it mean? ____ ____

- Read the words built on the root א מ ר.

וַיֹּאמַר   אָמַר   לֵאמֹר   וַיֹּאמֶר   תֹּאמְרוּן

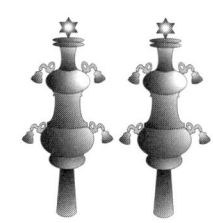

Verses from Parashat וַיִּשְׁלַח

Read these verses which describe Jacob's nighttime experience on his way home. Circle each word built on the root א מ ר.

1. וַיֹּאמֶר אֵלָיו מַה שְּׁמֶךָ וַיֹּאמֶר יַעֲקֹב.

And he [the man] said to him [Jacob]: "What is your name?" And he answered: "Jacob." (Genesis 32:28)

2. וַיֹּאמֶר לֹא יַעֲקֹב יֵאָמֵר עוֹד שִׁמְךָ כִּי אִם יִשְׂרָאֵל כִּי שָׂרִיתָ עִם אֱלֹהִים וְעִם אֲנָשִׁים וַתּוּכָל:

And he said: "Your name shall no longer be called Jacob, but Israel, because you have struggled with God and humans and you have won." (Genesis 32:29)

3. ...וַיֹּאמֶר הַגִּידָה נָּא שְׁמֶךָ...

...And he [Jacob] said [to the man]: "Please tell me your name."... (Genesis 32:30)

4. וַיִּקְרָא יַעֲקֹב שֵׁם הַמָּקוֹם פְּנִיאֵל...

And Jacob named the place Peniel: "Face of God"... (Genesis 32:31)

The Jewish people are sometimes called "Israel." What lesson do you think we can learn from our name, which was given as a result of determination and struggle?

____
____
____

What's in a Name?

One Hebrew name for God is אֵל. God's name is sometimes incorporated into other names. Read these names, then circle God's name in each one.

בֵּית־אֵל פְּנִיאֵל יִשְׂרָאֵל

1. One translation of יִשְׂרָאֵל is "one who struggled with God." What do you think was Jacob's true struggle with God?

_____

2. The name פְּנִיאֵל means "Face of God." Why do you think Jacob named the place where he wrestled פְּנִיאֵל?

_____

3. The name בֵּית־אֵל means "House of God." What two events happened in the place Jacob named בֵּית־אֵל?

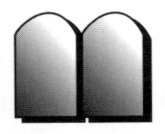

_____

Torah Fact

We say "Adonai" when we see God's name written as יהוה. We do not know how יהוה was originally pronounced. Sometimes *Adonai* is written in the siddur the way we pronounce it: אֲדוֹנָי. But usually it is written יְהֹוָה or יְיָ in the סִדּוּר and חֻמָּשׁ even though it is pronounced "*Adonai*."

Before each *aliyah* in the Torah reading, we recite the following blessing praising God for giving us the Torah. Practice the blessing.

בָּרְכוּ אֶת יְיָ הַמְבֹרָךְ.

בָּרוּךְ יְיָ הַמְבֹרָךְ לְעוֹלָם וָעֶד.

בָּרוּךְ אַתָּה, יְיָ אֱלֹהֵינוּ, מֶלֶךְ הָעוֹלָם, אֲשֶׁר בָּחַר בָּנוּ מִכָּל הָעַמִּים וְנָתַן לָנוּ אֶת תּוֹרָתוֹ. בָּרוּךְ אַתָּה, יְיָ, נוֹתֵן הַתּוֹרָה.

Praise Adonai, who is praiseworthy.
Praised is Adonai, who is praiseworthy forever and ever.
Praised are You, Adonai our God, Ruler of the universe, who chose us from all the nations and gave us the Torah. Praised are You, Adonai, who gives us the Torah.

Torah Reading

The following verses are taken from Genesis 32:28–31. They describe how Jacob wrestled with God, in the form of a man, who blessed him and renamed him Israel.

28
29 וַיֹּאמֶר אֵלָיו מַה שְּׁמֶךָ וַיֹּאמֶר יַעֲקֹב: וַיֹּאמֶר לֹא יַעֲקֹב יֵאָמֵר עוֹד שִׁמְךָ כִּי אִם יִשְׂרָאֵל כִּי שָׂרִיתָ עִם אֱלֹהִים וְעִם אֲנָשִׁים

30 וַתּוּכָל: וַיִּשְׁאַל יַעֲקֹב וַיֹּאמֶר הַגִּידָה נָּא שְׁמֶךָ וַיֹּאמֶר לָמָּה

31 זֶּה תִּשְׁאַל לִשְׁמִי וַיְבָרֶךְ אֹתוֹ שָׁם: וַיִּקְרָא יַעֲקֹב שֵׁם הַמָּקוֹם פְּנִיאֵל כִּי רָאִיתִי אֱלֹהִים פָּנִים אֶל פָּנִים וַתִּנָּצֵל נַפְשִׁי:

The Mitzvah Connection

Peace in the Home שְׁלוֹם בַּיִת

וַיָּרָץ עֵשָׂו לִקְרָאתוֹ וַיְחַבְּקֵהוּ...
וַיִּבְכּוּ:

And Esau ran to meet him, and embraced him…and they wept. (Genesis 33:4)

On Shabbat it is a special mitzvah to contribute to family peace and love. During the other days of the week there may be quarrels in our family. But on Shabbat, we make an extra effort to be considerate and thoughtful.

Read aloud the Hebrew verse and its English translation.

Peace in the home—שְׁלוֹם בַּיִת—is an important Jewish value. Our tradition encourages us to be kind, forgiving, and understanding to our loved ones.

Esau and Jacob wept when they embraced. Do you think it was easy for Esau to be forgiving? What do you think motivated him?

_____

_____

_____

_____

Think About It!

How can you add to שְׁלוֹם בַּיִת in your home?

✦ My Reflections on the Parashah ✦

בְּרֵאשִׁית נֹחַ לֶךְ־לְךָ וַיֵּרָא חַיֵּי שָׂרָה תּוֹלְדֹת
וַיֵּצֵא וַיִּשְׁלַח וַיֵּשֶׁב מִקֵּץ וַיִּגַּשׁ וַיְחִי

וַיֵּשֶׁב

Genesis 37:1–40:23

וַיֵּשֶׁב יַעֲקֹב בְּאֶרֶץ מְגוּרֵי אָבִיו בְּאֶרֶץ כְּנָעַן...וְיִשְׂרָאֵל אָהַב אֶת יוֹסֵף מִכָּל בָּנָיו כִּי בֶן זְקֻנִים הוּא לוֹ וְעָשָׂה לוֹ כְּתֹנֶת פַּסִּים:

Now Jacob settled in the land where his father had lived, in the land of Canaan…. And Israel loved Joseph more than all his children because he was the son of his old age, and he made him an ornamented coat. *(Genesis 37:1,3)*

Highlights from Parashat וַיֵּשֶׁב

Jacob and his family settled in Canaan. But there was no peace, for Jacob favored Joseph, the son of his old age, and Joseph would bring his father tales about his brothers. When Jacob gave Joseph an ornamented coat, his brothers' hatred of Joseph grew.

Joseph angered his brothers even more by telling them his dreams. In one dream, the brothers were all binding sheaves in the field. When Joseph's sheaf stood up, their sheaves bowed down to his. In the second dream, the sun and the moon (Joseph's father and mother) and eleven stars (his brothers) bowed down to Joseph.

One day, Jacob sent Joseph to see if all was well with his brothers and the flocks they were tending. When his brothers saw Joseph, they decided to kill him. They took off his ornamented coat and put him in a pit without water. Reuben and Judah convinced the other brothers not to kill Joseph. The brothers planned to sell him to a caravan of Ishmaelites. But, before they could do so, Midianite traders pulled Joseph out of the pit and sold him to the Ishmaelites, who brought him to Egypt.

The brothers dipped Joseph's coat in the blood of a goat and brought it to their father. Thinking that Joseph had been devoured by a beast, Jacob mourned for him.

In Egypt, Joseph was sold to Potiphar, Pharaoh's chief steward. Joseph lived in his master's house and was put in charge of the household. But Potiphar's wife was angered by him and, though innocent, he was sent to jail. Soon after Joseph was imprisoned, he was put in charge of the other prisoners.

Read the Verse

Read aloud the opening verse of *Parashat* וַיֵּשֶׁב and find the Hebrew word for which the *parashah* is named. Write the name of the *parashah*. _____

Torah Words

כְּתֹנֶת פַּסִּים — an ornamented coat

חֲלוֹם — a dream

מִצְרַיִם — Egypt

In Your Own Words
Read "Highlights from *Parashat* וַיֵּשֶׁב," then retell the story of Joseph and his brothers and the caravan using the Torah words above.

Think About It!
What was the significance of the brothers' taking Joseph's ornamented coat from him before throwing him into the pit?

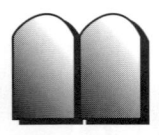

Torah Fact

סֵפֶר תּוֹרָה

רִמּוֹנִים

מְעִיל

חֹשֶׁן

יָד

We show our love and respect for the Torah by the way we dress the סֵפֶר תּוֹרָה. It is adorned at the top with a silver crown—כֶּתֶר תּוֹרָה—or silver rimmonim—רִמּוֹנִים. A beautiful cover called a mantle—מְעִיל—made of velvet or satin, is placed over the סֵפֶר תּוֹרָה and a silver breastplate—חֹשֶׁן—is placed over the mantle. Hanging down from one wooden roller is the pointer—יָד—which we use when we read from the סֵפֶר תּוֹרָה.

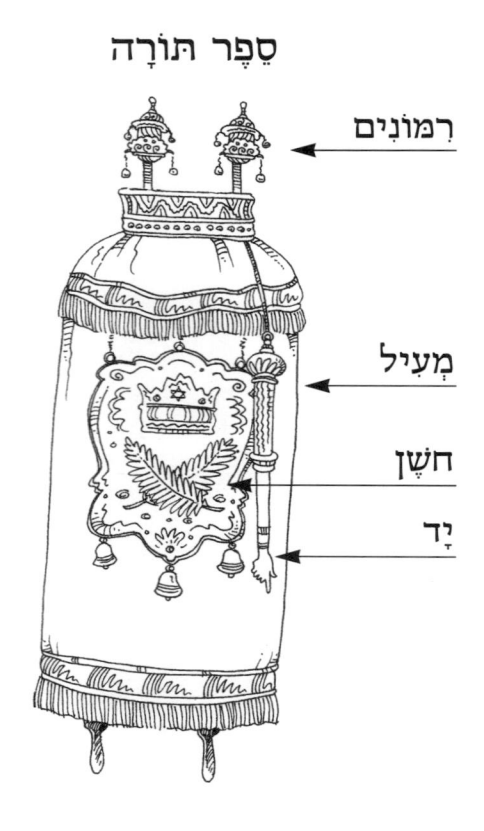

A Special Vowel

The vowel ָ makes the sound AW in כָל and כָּל. כָּל and כָל mean "all."

- Practice reading these words.

$$\text{בְּכָל} \quad \text{מִכָּל} \quad \text{וּבְכָל}$$

- Practice reading these phrases.

$$\text{מִכָּל בָּנָיו} \quad \text{מִכָּל אֶחָיו}$$

A Root: א ה ב

The root א ה ב means "love."

- Write the root. _____ _____ _____   What does it mean? _____

- Read the words built on the root א ה ב.

$$\text{אָהַב} \quad \text{אַהֲבָה} \quad \text{וְאָהַבְתָּ} \quad \text{אַהֲבַת}$$

- Add the word אָהַב to each verse below, and underline the English meaning of the word.

- Read the completed verses.

1. וְיִשְׂרָאֵל _____ אֶת יוֹסֵף מִכָּל בָּנָיו כִּי בֶן זְקֻנִים הוּא לוֹ...

   Israel loved Joseph more than all his children because he was the son of his old age...

   (Genesis 37:3)

2. וַיִּרְאוּ אֶחָיו כִּי אֹתוֹ _____ אֲבִיהֶם מִכָּל אֶחָיו וַיִּשְׂנְאוּ אֹתוֹ...

   When his brothers saw that their father loved him above all his brothers, they hated him...

   (Genesis 37:4)

Judaism teaches us not to go to extremes in our behavior, especially in our emotional responses. How does the story of Jacob and his children teach us that even feelings of love can have negative consequences when carried to an extreme?

_____

_____

Verses from Parashat וַיֵּשֶׁב

Read the text below in which Joseph describes his dreams.

1. וַיֹּאמֶר אֲלֵיהֶם שִׁמְעוּ נָא הַחֲלוֹם הַזֶּה אֲשֶׁר חָלָמְתִּי.

And he said to them [his brothers]: "Listen to the dream which I have dreamed." (Genesis 37:6)

2. ... תְסֻבֶּינָה אֲלֻמֹּתֵיכֶם וַתִּשְׁתַּחֲוֶיןָ לַאֲלֻמָּתִי.

"...your sheaves gathered around and were bowing down to my sheaf." (Genesis 37:7)

3. ... הַשֶּׁמֶשׁ וְהַיָּרֵחַ וְאַחַד עָשָׂר כּוֹכָבִים מִשְׁתַּחֲוִים לִי.

"...the sun and the moon and eleven stars bowed down to me." (Genesis 37:9)

Do you think Joseph was wise to share his dreams with his brothers? Explain your answer.

_____

_____

Torah Reading

The following verses are taken from Genesis 37:8–10. They describe how Joseph angered his family by telling them of a dream in which the sun, moon, and eleven stars bowed down to him.

8 וַיֹּאמְרוּ לוֹ אֶחָיו הֲמָלֹךְ תִּמְלֹךְ עָלֵינוּ אִם מָשׁוֹל תִּמְשֹׁל בָּנוּ

9 וַיּוֹסֶף עוֹד שְׂנֹא אֹתוֹ עַל חֲלֹמֹתָיו וְעַל דְּבָרָיו: וַיַּחֲלֹם עוֹד חֲלוֹם אַחֵר וַיְסַפֵּר אֹתוֹ לְאֶחָיו וַיֹּאמֶר הִנֵּה חָלַמְתִּי חֲלוֹם עוֹד

10 וְהִנֵּה הַשֶּׁמֶשׁ וְהַיָּרֵחַ וְאַחַד עָשָׂר כּוֹכָבִים מִשְׁתַּחֲוִים לִי: וַיְסַפֵּר אֶל אָבִיו וְאֶל אֶחָיו וַיִּגְעַר בּוֹ אָבִיו וַיֹּאמֶר לוֹ מָה הַחֲלוֹם הַזֶּה אֲשֶׁר חָלָמְתָּ...

The Mitzvah Connection

Guarding One's Tongue שְׁמִירַת הַלָּשׁוֹן

לֹא תֵלֵךְ רָכִיל בְּעַמֶּיךָ....

Do not go around as a talebearer among your people... (Leviticus 19:16)

A conversation may begin innocently enough. But sometimes, before we know it, we find ourselves gossiping or making an unkind comment about someone we don't like. How can we remind ourselves to guard our tongues instead?

Read aloud the Hebrew verse and its English translation. Joseph would bring his father bad reports about his brothers. How did Joseph's talebearing affect his relationship with his brothers? Why are tales and gossip harmful to the one who speaks them as well as those who are spoken about?

_____

_____

_____

_____

✦ My Reflections on the Parashah ✦

- Pharaoh had a wierd dream and the Chief Cupbearer remembered Joseph.
- Joseph said there would be seven years of plenty and 7 years of famine and Pharaoh put Joseph in charge of gathering and storing food.
- Jakob sent ten of his sons to Egypt and they saw Joseph and Joseph thought of a plan.
- Joseph accused his brothers of being spies and made them get Benjamin, he then accused Benjamin of theft after putting a cup in his sack.
- Joseph ignored his brothers plea to make Benjamin his slave.

בְּרֵאשִׁית נֹחַ לֶךְ-לְךָ וַיֵּרָא חַיֵּי שָׂרָה תּוֹלְדֹת
וַיֵּצֵא וַיִּשְׁלַח וַיֵּשֶׁב מִקֵּץ וַיִּגַּשׁ וַיְחִי

מִקֵּץ

Genesis 41:1–44:17

> וַיְהִי מִקֵּץ שְׁנָתַיִם יָמִים וּפַרְעֹה חֹלֵם וְהִנֵּה עֹמֵד עַל הַיְאֹר:
>
> And it came to pass at the end of two years, that Pharaoh dreamed: and behold he stood by the river Nile. *(Genesis 41:1)*

Highlights from Parashat מִקֵּץ

Pharaoh dreamed that he was standing by the Nile River. Nearby were seven strong cows and seven weak cows. The seven weak cows ate the seven strong cows. Pharaoh then dreamed of seven healthy ears of grain that grew on one stalk. Then, seven thin ears sprouted up and swallowed the healthy ears. The next day, hearing of Pharaoh's dreams, the chief cupbearer remembered Joseph and his gift for dreams.

Pharaoh sent for Joseph, who said that God was forewarning Pharaoh through his dreams that there would be seven years of plenty and seven years of famine. Pharaoh put Joseph in charge of gathering and storing food for the years of famine.

The famine was also in the land of Canaan. And Jacob sent ten of his sons down to Egypt to buy food. But he kept Benjamin, his youngest son, at home so that no harm would come to him. In Egypt, the brothers bowed down to Joseph (just as in his dreams), for they did not recognize him. But, Joseph recognized them and devised a plan of trickery.

Joseph did not reveal himself. He accused his brothers of being spies and required them to bring their youngest brother (Benjamin), whom they had spoken of, to Egypt to prove their innocence. Though it grieved Jacob to let Benjamin go, the famine was great and the family needed food. So, Benjamin went down to Egypt with his brothers. Joseph had his steward secretly place a silver goblet in Benjamin's sack. Later Joseph accused him of theft.

When the goblet was discovered, the brothers returned to Joseph but still did not recognize him. Joseph ignored the pleas of Judah, who spoke on behalf of his brothers, and said that Benjamin was to become his slave, while the other brothers were to return to their father.

Read the Verse

Read aloud the opening verse of *Parashat* מִקֵּץ and find the Hebrew word for which the *parashah* is named. Write the name of the *parashah*. _____

Torah Words

שִׁבֳּלִים
grain

פָּרוֹת
cows

פַּרְעֹה
Pharaoh

In Your Own Words
Read "Highlights from *Parashat* מִקֵּץ," then retell Pharaoh's dream using the Torah words above.

A Special Vowel

The vowel ֳ makes the sound AW. Read the phrases below.

כָּל שִׁבֳּלִים   כָּל הַשִׁבֳּלִים

A Root: ר ע ב

The root ר ע ב means "hunger" and "famine."

- Write the root. ____ ____ ____   What does it mean? _____ _____

- Read the words built on the root ר ע ב.

וַתִּרְעַב   רַעֲבוֹן   רָעָב

- Add the root letters ר ע ב to complete the word in each verse.

- Underline the English translation of each completed word, then read the Hebrew.

1. וַתִּ_ְ_ַ_ כָּל אֶרֶץ מִצְרַיִם וַיִּצְעַק הָעָם אֶל פַּרְעֹה לַלָּחֶם...

And when all the land of Egypt felt the famine, the people cried out to Pharaoh for bread...
(Genesis 41:55)

2. וְהָ_ָ_ָ_ הָיָה עַל כָּל פְּנֵי הָאָרֶץ...

And the famine was over all the earth... (Genesis 41:56)

Word Watch

Read each Hebrew phrase and its English translation.

שֶׁבַע שִׁבֳּלִים	שֶׁבַע פָּרוֹת	שֶׁבַע שְׁנֵי רָעָב	שֶׁבַע שָׁנִים	שֶׁבַע שָׁנִים
seven ears of grain	seven cows	seven years of famine	seven years	

Which word is repeated in each Hebrew phrase? _____ What does it mean? _____ Watch for the word patterns in the verses that follow.

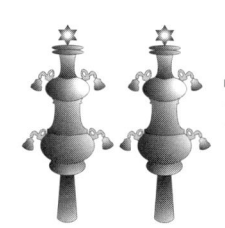

Verses from Parashat מִקֵּץ

Read Pharaoh's description of his dreams.

1. וַתֹּאכַלְנָה הַפָּרוֹת הָרַקּוֹת וְהָרָעוֹת
   אֵת שֶׁבַע הַפָּרוֹת הָרִאשֹׁנוֹת הַבְּרִיאֹת.
   "And the lean and ugly cows ate up the first seven healthy cows." (Genesis 41:20)

2. וַתִּבְלַעְןָ הַשִּׁבֳּלִים הַדַּקֹּת אֵת שֶׁבַע הַשִׁבֳּלִים הַטֹּבוֹת...
   "And the thin ears of grain swallowed up the seven good ears..." (Genesis 41:24)

Read Joseph's interpretation of Pharaoh's dreams.

3. שֶׁבַע פָּרֹת הַטֹּבֹת שֶׁבַע שָׁנִים הֵנָּה
   וְשֶׁבַע הַשִׁבֳּלִים הַטֹּבֹת שֶׁבַע שָׁנִים...
   "The seven good cows are seven years and the seven good ears [of grain] are seven years..." (Genesis 41:26)

4. וְשֶׁבַע הַפָּרוֹת הָרַקּוֹת וְהָרָעֹת...שֶׁבַע שָׁנִים הֵנָּה
   וְשֶׁבַע הַשִׁבֳּלִים הָרֵקוֹת...יִהְיוּ שֶׁבַע שְׁנֵי רָעָב.
   "The seven lean and ugly cows...are seven years. Also the seven empty ears...will be seven years of famine." (Genesis 41:27)

Joseph's misfortunes began when he shared his dreams of ruling over his family. They ended when he interpreted Pharaoh's dreams and worked for the welfare of others. What lesson about how to use our talents can we learn from this Bible story?

_____

_____

_____

Torah Fact

At the conclusion of each *aliyah* in the Torah reading we recite a blessing. Practice reading the blessing.

בָּרוּךְ אַתָּה, יְיָ אֱלֹהֵינוּ, מֶלֶךְ הָעוֹלָם,

אֲשֶׁר נָתַן לָנוּ תּוֹרַת אֱמֶת וְחַיֵּי עוֹלָם נָטַע בְּתוֹכֵנוּ.

בָּרוּךְ אַתָּה, יְיָ, נוֹתֵן הַתּוֹרָה.

Praised are You, Adonai our God, Ruler of the universe,
who gave us the Torah of truth and planted within us eternal life.
Praised are You, Adonai, who gives us the Torah.

Think About It!
What do you think the phrase "planted within us eternal life" means?

Torah Reading

The following verses are taken from Genesis 41:26–30. They describe how Joseph explained that Pharaoh's dreams foretold seven years of plenty and seven years of famine in Egypt.

26 שֶׁבַע פָּרֹת הַטֹּבֹת שֶׁבַע שָׁנִים הֵנָּה וְשֶׁבַע הַשִּׁבֳּלִים הַטֹּבֹת שֶׁבַע

27 שָׁנִים הֵנָּה חֲלוֹם אֶחָד הוּא: וְשֶׁבַע הַפָּרוֹת הָרַקּוֹת וְהָרָעֹת

הָעֹלֹת אַחֲרֵיהֶן שֶׁבַע שָׁנִים הֵנָּה וְשֶׁבַע הַשִּׁבֳּלִים הָרֵקוֹת

28 שְׁדֻפוֹת הַקָּדִים יִהְיוּ שֶׁבַע שְׁנֵי רָעָב: הוּא הַדָּבָר אֲשֶׁר דִּבַּרְתִּי

29 אֶל פַּרְעֹה אֲשֶׁר הָאֱלֹהִים עֹשֶׂה הֶרְאָה אֶת פַּרְעֹה: הִנֵּה שֶׁבַע

30 שָׁנִים בָּאוֹת שָׂבָע גָּדוֹל בְּכָל אֶרֶץ מִצְרָיִם: וְקָמוּ שֶׁבַע שְׁנֵי

רָעָב אַחֲרֵיהֶן...

The Mitzvah Connection

Feeding the Hungry מַאֲכִיל רְעֵבִים

וְתָפֵק לָרָעֵב נַפְשֶׁךָ
וְנֶפֶשׁ נַעֲנָה תַּשְׂבִּיעַ
וְזָרַח בַּחֹשֶׁךְ אוֹרֶךָ
וַאֲפֵלָתְךָ כַּצָּהֳרָיִם.

*If you give your attention to the hungry,
And feed the oppressed people,
Then your light will shine in darkness,
And your darkness will become noontime.*

(Isaiah 58:10)

The members of this synagogue are packing canned foods to be distributed to those in need.

Read aloud the Hebrew verse and its English translation. How can you add light to your community by performing the מִצְוָה of מַאֲכִיל רְעֵבִים?

_____

_____

Think About It!

Why does our tradition teach that *feeling* compassion is not enough to bring light into the world? We must *act* with righteousness. We must perform מִצְוֹת, acts of holiness, such as מַאֲכִיל רְעֵבִים.

✦ **My Reflections on the Parashah** ✦

בְּרֵאשִׁית נֹחַ לֶךְ־לְךָ וַיֵּרָא חַיֵּי שָׂרָה תּוֹלְדֹת
וַיֵּצֵא וַיִּשְׁלַח וַיֵּשֶׁב מִקֵּץ וַיִּגַּשׁ וַיְחִי

וַיִּגַּשׁ

Genesis 44:18–47:27

וַיִּגַּשׁ אֵלָיו יְהוּדָה וַיֹּאמֶר בִּי אֲדֹנִי יְדַבֶּר נָא עַבְדְּךָ דָבָר בְּאָזְנֵי אֲדֹנִי... יֶשׁ לָנוּ אָב זָקֵן וְיֶלֶד זְקֻנִים קָטָן וְאָחִיו מֵת וַיִּוָּתֵר הוּא לְבַדּוֹ לְאִמּוֹ וְאָבִיו אֲהֵבוֹ:

Then Judah approached him and said, "Please, my lord, let your servant have a word with my lord…. [We told my lord,] 'We have an old father with a child of his old age, the youngest; and his brother is dead so that he alone is left of his mother, and his father loves him.'" *(Genesis 44:18,20)*

Highlights from Parashat וַיִּגַּשׁ

Despairing that Joseph threatened to make a slave of Benjamin, Judah pleaded with Joseph. He spoke of Jacob's agony over sending Benjamin down to Egypt and explained that if they now were to return without Benjamin, their father would surely die of grief. Judah asked that Joseph accept him as a slave in place of Benjamin.

Overcome by emotion, Joseph revealed himself to his brothers and told them not to fear him. He reassured them that they were not responsible for what happened in the past; rather, it was God who sent him to Egypt in order to save their lives in the time of the famine. At Joseph's direction, the brothers returned to Canaan and told their father that Joseph was alive and was a ruler over Egypt. They explained that Joseph wanted Jacob and his entire family to join him and settle in the region of Goshen.

Jacob set out on the journey. When he reached Beer Sheba, God called out to him in another nighttime vision telling him not to fear going down to Egypt for God would make him into a great nation there. God said, "I will go with you to Egypt, and I will also bring you back." Joseph met his father in Goshen. They hugged and wept. Pharaoh greeted Joseph's family warmly, offering them the best of his land. And the family of Jacob settled there and increased greatly.

Read the Verse

Read aloud the opening verse of *Parashat* וַיִּגַּשׁ and find the Hebrew word for which the *parashah* is named. Write the name of the *parashah*. _____

Torah Words

אָבִיו	יַעֲקֹב	אֶחָיו	יוֹסֵף
his father	Jacob	his brothers	Joseph

In Your Own Words

Read "Highlights from *Parashat* וַיִּגַּשׁ." Describe the relationship between Joseph and his father and the changes in the relationship between Joseph and his brothers. Use the Torah words above in your descriptions.

Double-Duty Dot

Sometimes the dot in the letter שׁ is also the "O" vowel for the preceding letter. Read each word below.

מֹשֶׁה   שָׁלֹשׁ   קָדֹשׁ   חֹשֶׁךְ   גֹּשֶׁן   חֹשֶׁן

Biblical Geography

Write the correct English name under each Hebrew name.

Goshen	Haran	Egypt	Canaan
כְּנַעַן	מִצְרַיִם	גֹּשֶׁן	חָרָן
_____	_____	_____	_____

Next to each description of a place, write the Hebrew name of the place.

1. This is the land of our ancestors. It is now called Israel. _____

2. Joseph rose to a high position in this land. _____

3. Jacob's uncle Laban lived here. _____

4. Joseph settled his family in this region. _____

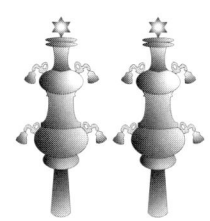

Verses from Parashiyot וַיֵּצֵא, וַיִּשְׁלַח, וַיִּגַּשׁ

Read about Jacob's three encounters with God.

Parashat וַיֵּצֵא

Jacob left בְּאֵר שֶׁבַע to journey toward Ḥaran. He planned to find a wife among the daughters of his uncle, Laban. He rested on the way to Ḥaran and had a dream that angels of God were ascending and descending a ladder. Jacob understood that he had encountered God in the night.

וְהִנֵּה אָנֹכִי עִמָּךְ וּשְׁמַרְתִּיךָ בְּכֹל אֲשֶׁר תֵּלֵךְ וַהֲשִׁבֹתִיךָ אֶל הָאֲדָמָה הַזֹּאת...

[God said]: "I am with you and will protect you wherever you go and will bring you back to this land..." (Genesis 28:15)

Parashat וַיִּשְׁלַח

Twenty years later Jacob took his wives, his children, and all he possessed and journeyed back to his father in כְּנַעַן. He wrestled with "a man" during the night and won. At dawn the man changed Jacob's name to Israel. Jacob understood that he had encountered God in the night.

...כִּי רָאִיתִי אֱלֹהִים פָּנִים אֶל פָּנִים וַתִּנָּצֵל נַפְשִׁי.

"...For I have seen God face to face and my life has been spared." (Genesis 32:31)

Parashat וַיִּגַּשׁ

Jacob, now an old man, set out for מִצְרַיִם to be reunited with Joseph. He came to בְּאֵר שֶׁבַע, the place he had left so many years before when he traveled to Ḥaran. Jacob heard the voice of God in visions as he slept.

וַיֹּאמֶר אֱלֹהִים לְיִשְׂרָאֵל...וַיֹּאמֶר יַעֲקֹב יַעֲקֹב וַיֹּאמֶר הִנֵּנִי. וַיֹּאמֶר אָנֹכִי הָאֵל אֱלֹהֵי אָבִיךָ... אָנֹכִי אֵרֵד עִמְּךָ מִצְרַיְמָה וְאָנֹכִי אַעַלְךָ גַם עָלֹה....

And God spoke to Israel...and said: "Jacob, Jacob." And he [Jacob] said: "Here I am." And [God] said: "I am God, the God of your father.... I will go down with you to Egypt, and I will also bring you back up again..." (Genesis 46:2–4)

Practice reading the verses in Hebrew, then answer the questions on page 70.

1. What do you think the significance is of Jacob's encountering God while on a journey?

_____

_____

2. What relationship developed between God and Jacob in the course of the three encounters?

_____

_____

The Children of Jacob

Jacob had twelve sons, and one daughter named דִינָה.

Read aloud the Hebrew names of Jacob's twelve sons, which are listed from the oldest, רְאוּבֵן, to the youngest, בִּנְיָמִין.

The Twelve Tribes of Israel were made up of descendants of the sons of Jacob.

Next to each English name, write the number of the matching Hebrew name.

_____ Zebulun
_____ Levi
_____ Issachar
_____ Reuben
_____ Judah
_____ Asher
_____ Naphtali
_____ Simeon
_____ Joseph
_____ Gad
_____ Benjamin
_____ Dan

1. רְאוּבֵן
2. שִׁמְעוֹן
3. לֵוִי
4. יְהוּדָה
5. דָן
6. נַפְתָּלִי
7. גָד
8. אָשֵׁר
9. יִשָּׂשכָר
10. זְבֻלוּן
11. יוֹסֵף
12. בִּנְיָמִין

Torah Reading

The following verses are taken from Genesis 45:12–15. They describe how Joseph and Benjamin were reunited.

12 וְהִנֵּה עֵינֵיכֶם רֹאוֹת וְעֵינֵי אָחִי בִנְיָמִין כִּי פִי הַמְדַבֵּר אֲלֵיכֶם:
13 וְהִגַּדְתֶּם לְאָבִי אֶת כָּל כְּבוֹדִי בְּמִצְרַיִם וְאֵת כָּל אֲשֶׁר רְאִיתֶם
14 וּמִהַרְתֶּם וְהוֹרַדְתֶּם אֶת אָבִי הֵנָּה: וַיִּפֹּל עַל צַוְּארֵי בִנְיָמִן
15 אָחִיו וַיֵּבְךְּ וּבִנְיָמִן בָּכָה עַל צַוָּארָיו: וַיְנַשֵּׁק לְכָל אֶחָיו וַיֵּבְךְּ עֲלֵהֶם וְאַחֲרֵי כֵן דִּבְּרוּ אֶחָיו אִתּוֹ:

The Mitzvah Connection

Forgiveness סְלִיחָה

אֲנִי יוֹסֵף...וְלֹא יָכְלוּ אֶחָיו לַעֲנוֹת אֹתוֹ כִּי נִבְהֲלוּ מִפָּנָיו. וַיֹּאמֶר יוֹסֵף...גְּשׁוּ נָא אֵלַי...וְעַתָּה אַל תֵּעָצְבוּ וְאַל יִחַר בְּעֵינֵיכֶם...

"I am Joseph."... And his brothers could not answer him, for they were frightened by being in his presence. And Joseph said: "...Draw near me.... Do not be distressed and do not be angry with yourselves...." (Genesis 45:3–5)

This boy's grandmother was hurt when he spoke disrespectfully. What might the boy have done to gain his grandmother's forgiveness? Do you think the grandmother was right to forgive the boy? Why or why not?

Read aloud the Hebrew verses and the English translation. In this passage, Joseph reveals who he is to his brothers and reassures them that they need not be afraid. All that happened, he says, was part of God's plan so that he would be in a position to save lives. Jewish tradition emphasizes not only the importance of apologizing for our mistakes but also the importance of forgiving those who have wronged us. How can developing the quality of forgiveness make us into better people?

_____

_____

_____

✦ **My Reflections on the Parashah** ✦

בְּרֵאשִׁית נֹחַ לֶךְ־לְךָ וַיֵּרָא חַיֵּי שָׂרָה תּוֹלְדֹת
וַיֵּצֵא וַיִּשְׁלַח וַיֵּשֶׁב מִקֵּץ וַיִּגַּשׁ וַיְחִי

וַיְחִי

Genesis 47:28–50:26

וַיְחִי יַעֲקֹב בְּאֶרֶץ מִצְרַיִם שְׁבַע עֶשְׂרֵה שָׁנָה וַיְהִי יְמֵי יַעֲקֹב שְׁנֵי חַיָּיו שֶׁבַע שָׁנִים וְאַרְבָּעִים וּמְאַת שָׁנָה: וַיִּקְרְבוּ יְמֵי יִשְׂרָאֵל לָמוּת...

And Jacob lived in the land of Egypt 17 years, and his life spanned 147 years. The time drew near for Israel to die… *(Genesis 47:28–29)*

Highlights from Parashat וַיְחִי

When Jacob [Israel] was 147 years old, he asked Joseph to bury him in the land of Canaan when he died. Joseph swore he would fulfill his father's request. Later, weakened by illness, Jacob blessed Joseph and his sons, Ephraim and Manasseh, who had come to be with him.

Jacob's and Joseph's sons became the leaders of the Twelve Tribes of Israel. Jacob called his sons to him, spoke of each one's destiny based on his character, and gave his blessings. He praised Judah as the strongest leader and called Joseph the "elect of his brothers." According to one interpretation of the text, Jacob said that the blessings he bestowed on Joseph greatly exceeded those that he, Jacob, had received from his ancestors.

Jacob instructed his sons to bury him in the cave in the field of Machpelah, the cave in which Abraham and Sarah, Isaac and Rebecca, and Jacob's wife Leah were buried. Then Jacob died.

Joseph grieved deeply for Jacob. He asked for Pharaoh's permission to go to Canaan to bury his father, promising to return to Egypt. On the journey with his brothers and officials from Pharaoh's court, Joseph stopped and mourned his father for seven days. Then, just as Isaac and Ishmael had buried Abraham, and Jacob and Esau had buried Isaac, so too did Joseph and his brothers bury Jacob.

With their father dead, Joseph's brothers once again feared that Joseph would seek revenge. But he reassured them that he would take care of them and their families. Joseph was 110 years old when he died. Before he died, he asked that his remains be taken to Canaan, the land God had promised to Abraham, Isaac, and Jacob. (Joseph was buried first in Egypt. Later, the Bible tells us, his bones were taken out of Egypt by Moses [Exodus 13:19] and buried in Canaan by Joshua [Joshua 24:32].)

Read the Verse

Read aloud the opening verse of *Parashat* וַיְחִי and find the Hebrew word for which the *parashah* is named. Write the name of the *parashah*. _____

Torah Words

וּקְבַרְתַּנִי בִּקְבֻרָתָם
and bury me in their burial-place

In Your Own Words
Read "Highlights from *Parashat* וַיְחִי." Imagine that you are Jacob as he is about to die. Speaking as Jacob, explain why you want to be buried in the same place as your father and mother (Isaac and Rebecca), your grandfather and grandmother (Abraham and Sarah), and your wife (Leah). Use the Torah phrase above in your explanation.

Think About It!
Like our ancestors, today many families have family burial plots so that family members can be buried in the same place. Why do you think this is important to families?

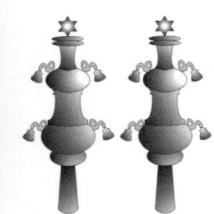

Verses from Parashat וַיְחִי

Read these verses from *Parashat* וַיְחִי, and then answer the questions.

1. וְשָׁכַבְתִּי עִם אֲבֹתַי וּנְשָׂאתַנִי מִמִּצְרַיִם... הִשָּׁבְעָה לִי וַיִּשָּׁבַע לוֹ...

"When I [Jacob] lie down with my ancestors, carry me out of Egypt...swear to me," and he [Joseph] swore to him... (Genesis 47:30–31)

- What does Jacob mean when he says, "When I lie down..."? _____

- Why do you think he wants to return to Canaan? _____

2. וַיַּשְׁבַּע יוֹסֵף אֶת בְּנֵי יִשְׂרָאֵל לֵאמֹר פָּקֹד יִפְקֹד אֱלֹהִים אֶתְכֶם וְהַעֲלִתֶם אֶת עַצְמֹתַי מִזֶּה: וַיָּמָת יוֹסֵף...

And Joseph made the children of Israel swear, saying: "God surely will remember you, so you shall carry my bones up from here." Then Joseph died. (Genesis 50:25–26)

- Joseph had been protecting and caring for his brothers and their families. What reassurance is he giving them when he tells them that God will remember them?

Joseph's Sons

Joseph had two sons. The older son was מְנַשֶּׁה and the younger אֶפְרַיִם. They are remembered by Jewish tradition as brothers who got along in every way. Jacob blessed them both saying:

וַיְבָרְכֵם בַּיּוֹם הַהוּא לֵאמוֹר בְּךָ יְבָרֵךְ יִשְׂרָאֵל לֵאמֹר
יְשִׂמְךָ אֱלֹהִים כְּאֶפְרַיִם וְכִמְנַשֶּׁה...

And he blessed them that day, saying: "In your name shall the people of Israel invoke this blessing—May God make you like Ephraim and like Manasseh..." (Genesis 48:20)

Think About It!

Why might Jacob have chosen Ephraim and Manasseh to create a link with future generations?

A Shabbat Blessing

Traditionally, a blessing is recited on Shabbat for sons and for daughters. Jacob's blessing became the blessing for sons. The blessing for daughters reflects the lives of our matriarchs. Recite each blessing.

יְשִׂמְךָ אֱלֹהִים כְּאֶפְרַיִם וְכִמְנַשֶּׁה.

May God make you like Ephraim and like Manasseh.

יְשִׂמֵךְ אֱלֹהִים כְּשָׂרָה, רִבְקָה, רָחֵל, וְלֵאָה.

May God make you like Sarah, Rebecca, Rachel, and Leah.

Think About It!

With what qualities of the matriarchs might parents want their daughters to be blessed?

Torah Reading

The following verses are taken from Genesis 50:14–17. They describe how Joseph's brothers once again feared that Joseph would seek revenge, now that their father was dead.

14 וַיָּשָׁב יוֹסֵף מִצְרַיְמָה הוּא וְאֶחָיו וְכָל הָעֹלִים אִתּוֹ לִקְבֹּר
15 אֶת אָבִיו אַחֲרֵי קָבְרוֹ אֶת אָבִיו: וַיִּרְאוּ אֲחֵי יוֹסֵף כִּי מֵת אֲבִיהֶם וַיֹּאמְרוּ לוּ יִשְׂטְמֵנוּ יוֹסֵף וְהָשֵׁב יָשִׁיב לָנוּ אֵת כָּל
16 הָרָעָה אֲשֶׁר גָּמַלְנוּ אֹתוֹ: וַיְצַוּוּ אֶל יוֹסֵף לֵאמֹר אָבִיךָ צִוָּה לִפְנֵי
17 מוֹתוֹ לֵאמֹר: כֹּה תֹאמְרוּ לְיוֹסֵף אָנָּא שָׂא נָא פֶּשַׁע אַחֶיךָ וְחַטָּאתָם כִּי רָעָה גְמָלוּךָ...

The Mitzvah Connection

The Study of Torah תַּלְמוּד תּוֹרָה

לְדָגִים אֵין חַיִּים בְּלִי מַיִם
וְאֵין חַיִּים בְּלִי תּוֹרָה לַיְּהוּדִים.

For fish there is no life without water, and there is no life without Torah for the Jewish people. (Parable from Rabbi Akiva)

Studying to become a bar or bat mitzvah provides a foundation for a lifetime of learning. Just as we reread the Torah year after year in synagogue, so our tradition teaches us to continue our Jewish studies throughout our lives.

Read aloud the Hebrew verse and the English translation. Do you think the Torah can be the source of life for the Jewish people if only religious leaders, such as rabbis and cantors, study it? Give reasons for your answer.

_____

_____

_____

Torah Fact

We have completed the study of the Book of Genesis. In a synagogue, the congregation traditionally says the words below when a book of Torah is completed. Let us say these words together.

$$\text{חֲזַק חֲזַק וְנִתְחַזֵּק}$$

Be strong, be strong, and let us strengthen one another.

✦ *Mitzvah Journal* ✦